THE COMPLETE
HISTORY AND
PHILOSOPHY OF
KUNG FU

THE COMPLETE HISTORY AND PHILOSOPHY OF KUNG FU

Dr. Earl C. Medeiros

Illustrated by Ed Lidinsky

Charles E. Tuttle Co., Inc.
Rutland, Vermont 05701

Representatives
Continental Europe: BOXERBOOKS, INC., Zurich
British Isles: PRENTICE-HALL INTERNATIONAL, INC., London
Australasia: PAUL FLESCH & CO., PTY. LTD., Melbourne
Canada: HURTIG PUBLISHERS, Edmonton, Alberta

Published by the Charles E. Tuttle Co., Inc.
of Rutland, Vermont, U.S.A.
with editorial offices at Suido 1-chome,
Bunkyo-ku, Tokyo, Japan

Library of Congress Catalog
Card No. 74-27619
International Standard Book No. 0-8048-1148-2

The Complete History and Philosophy of Kung Fu

FOREWORD

The art of Kung Fu has, at long last, gained true recognition as the highest form of the martial arts. It has gained acceptance and prominence in the eyes of the western world. Due to its meteoric rise, owing much to the impetus given by the commercial world in the form of television and movies, there have been a few attempts to define the arts; and in many cases these authors have less than a cursory aquaintance with Kung Fu. As a result of this limited background, much of the information is at best sparse. Having invested much time and effort in researching the many ramifications of Kung Fu, I feel that you, the reader, should be initiated into the art with a clear understanding of what Kung Fu really is.

Though our concern is primarily Kung Fu, it is impossible to fully appreciate the evolution of this art form without a complete perspective of Chinese Boxing as a whole, i.e., the philosophical, physiological and the historical implications which have helped to mold the art into the sophisticated structure it is today.

I have attempted to organize the available fragmentary information which consists of legend, hearsay, and to some degree fact; and to give this data some degree of chronological continuity. However, because of the variations in translation from the original Chinese, as well as the lack of recorded and reliable information, there is many times a disagreement of names and dates. I have attempted to use those references which are agreed upon by the majority of authors.

Researching the following data has been a most enjoyable and informative experience. I hope it is equally enjoyable and informative to the reader.

INTRODUCTION

Throughout the ages, man has sought an answer to the mysteries of life. He has sought to establish an identity with the cosmology and order of things. Always, he has sought to discover a philosophy which will serve all his needs and satisfy his endless thirst for knowledge, his reason for being, his reason for dying.

He has made attempt after attempt to discover the answer to many of these questions, however, has either been unsuccessful or has developed only one aspect of the total philosophy. Too often, he has lost perspective of the necessary harmony between mind and body as total oneness of man. And so he has leaned toward developing either one or the other and so has been unable to discover a philosophy which embraces both the mind and the body. . . . each in perfect harmony with the other and both in keeping with the laws of nature. These laws dictate that evolution takes place in keeping with the natural law . . . that they develop unopposed, unrestricted, smoothly, fluidly, and in keeping with the natural order of things. For centuries, religion under one guise or another, provided answers for many people to many questions. It, many times, demanded acceptance on the basis of blind faith. Also, more frequently than not, it proposed solutions which were in direct opposition to nature or to the natural laws. As a result, the significance of religion as a driving force slowly waned. With the advent of science and the fantastic contributions and discoveries, the position of religion has become less and less the answer to man's needs.

Once again, fulfillment in these areas satisfies only one segment of man's total make-up. Remembering that he is a two-dimensional animal, we have established a disharmony and therefore a contradiction of the natural law.

Kung Fu represents the natural development of man as a complete person. It develops both the spiritual and/or mental and the physical. It offers the answers that attract many people to psychiatrists, religion and sometimes to their own souls in search of their identity and of inner peace. It combines the theological with the philosophical and blends these with the physical, thus evolving those attitutudes which are in keeping with the natural laws. King Fu is a perfect harmony of mind and body, the physical with the metaphysical. . . . all in one . . . with no contradictions. The principles are valid throughout the whole philosophy. It is a circle within a circle. The more one sees, the more one wants to see; the more one learns, the more one wants to learn. It is an unending cycle of questions and answers. Each answer is complete but not final, because each answer gives rise to another question . . . and so learning and improvement flow ceaselessly like a natural, uninterrupted, rippling, clear stream.

Kung Fu develops man as a man . . . total and complete. It suppresses the basic, hostile, aggressive instincts and restores his nature to the basic simple, natural attitude of an unspoiled child . . . an uncarved block. It teaches us to walk again with our head up high; to be good, not bad; to be friendly, not callous; to be soft, not hard; to be happy and fulfilled. It is a philosophy of life and/or religion.

It develops the physical attitude through a form of exercises which are synonomous with the ultimate weapon of self-defense, because unlike other martial arts, the principles of Kung Fu are in keeping with the natural laws stressing softness, not hardness; yielding, not aggression; contentment, not frustration. It develops the mental, and philosophical and/or spiritual by cultivating a spirit of inward serenity and mental tranquility, thereby establishing a calmness of mind that puts the body into a relaxed state of equilibrium.

To further consider the physical aspect, practicality dictates that we approach this proposition with the consideration of not only self-defense but also health and longevity. There are two ways to reach our objective.

The first is the approach advocated by most sports, competetive organizations or other martial arts. The rule is the development of speed and strength. The regimen often includes weight lifting, running, speed techniques and other strenuous physical disciplines which increase bulk, strength, stamina, and the development of hypertrophic musculature. All this predicated on the false assumption that the strongest and the fastest always win. We can readily see the results of such a program. Our football and baseball heroes, and many of the good fighters in some martial arts seldom last for four or five peak years. Unfortunately everyone ages, and with age comes a decrease in the efficiency of the machinery needed to maintain these standards . . . musculature sags, strength ebbs, and speed decreases.

On the other hand, how can one account for many old men in China, some as old as 75, who are still able to throw through the air, men one third their ages, with twice their strength and twice their size. The answer is simple. Through proper training to develop the soft rather than the hard, the yielding rather than the resistant, and a cultivation of inner strength based on the utilization of root and reinforced with ch'i, these old masters are still capable of performing as well as the young athelete.

Kung Fu, properly taught and properly learned, is

truly the mother source of all self defense. All its movements and postures represent a form of martial art superior to all others. But most important, it is the perfect philosophical union of mind and body, thus giving rise to the perfect harmony of both aspects of man's nature and therefore evolving the development of man as a whole, poised, confident, harmonious complete being.

Kung Fu is a perfect harmony of mind and body . . .
. . . as a scale in perfect balance.

This is Kung Fu

Of all the words in the English language, few today have retained the meaning originally associated with them. Because of common usage, bombardment with familiarity, colloquial affectations, and facility of adaptability, many words have undergone transmutation of one kind or another. So too with the Chinese language. Many words have lost their original meaning and have come to be used in a manner contrary to their original meaning.

Many years ago, during the period of Chinese history when chemistry was still clouded with mystique, Kung Fu was a term designated to the alchemists. They labored long hours, and expended much time and energy in the pursuit of their objectives, and so they were spoken of as being possessed with Kung Fu. With usage the term became applicable to anyone who had devoted much time and energy in the aquisition of knowledge and proficiency in any art. Wu Shu, a generalized term for the practice of the martial arts required much time and energy before one became proficient, and eventually the term Kung Fu, became a colloqualism used in reference to any of the martial arts.

Because of the difference in dialect, the pronunciation was altered and in the Mandarin area Kung Fu was prevalent, while in the Cantonese region, Gung Fu was used. The term has been transported to the western world as being synonymous with any of the martial arts.

To properly define Kung Fu, thus giving it the real meaning, we must consider the three-fold aspect of the art . . . i.e., self-defense, philosophical, and health.

In so far as all three of these elements are involved in the development of Kung Fu, it is necessary to relate these aspects to the overall picture.

The development of Kung Fu arose out of a need of the times, for fighting is as old as man himself. Instinctively man depended on his hands and feet to battle the elements. As time passed, it underwent many years of refinement until it reached the high level of sophistication attained under the Chinese influence. In China, coupled with a deep concern for hygiene and longevity, plus the philosophical tide that was sweeping the country, martial arts attained a level of perfection that was to influence all countries for years to follow.

Kung Fu is the product of several thousand years of Chinese civilization. Its psychological and physiological aspects are founded on a profound and ancient philosophy which dates back to the period of the Yellow Emperor (2696 B.C.) and his influence on hygiene. Initially it was designed for the promotion of health through a harmony of the mind and body. Towards this end, the ancients designed a system of ballet-like calisthenics which were effortless and rhythmical, stressing proper breathing, balance, and relaxed postures resulting in absolute calmness of the mind, the pliability of a child, the strength of a lumberjack, and the peace of mind of a sage.

These principles were supported heavily by philosophical concepts such as Lao Tzu's Taoism and the I-Ching or the Book of Change.

The Taoist doctrine of naturalism and the Chinese concept of the universe as well as the doctrine of change, are reflected in the character of Kung Fu to no small degree.

1. The Principle of Continuity and Wholeness . . .

according to Taoism, the universe is an organic whole, an extensive continuum of interrelationships. There are no isolated parts. Also it is a dynamic universe which is governed by a continuous interaction of two opposite attributes which are separate and unique, yet interdependent and co-existent in their unity through a harmonious interaction. These same principles are applicable to the practice of Kung Fu. No part of the body acts independently. The whole body acts as one piece, united, inseparable. The constant change of the universe resembles the movements of Kung Fu which are uninterrupted, flowing, no breaks or gaps . . . the end of one move is not an end, but the beginning of the next move.

2. Principle of Contrasts in Harmony . . . according to the ancient Chinese, the universe is made up through the interaction of two forces, Yin and Yang. Their counterparts are hard and soft, cold and warm, solid and empty, night and day. This personalization of the universe is the process of harmonizing contrasts into one unity. Kung Fu is also designed for the harmony of mind and body. Unlike most schools, Kung Fu is not dependent on strength, force and bravery, but rather on a balance of mind and body, so that the mind strengthens, fortifies, and directs the body. Also there is a succession of opposite movements, so that the hand which is above, descends and the hand which is down, rises. The leg bearing the weight, becomes empty, while the leg which was empty becomes real. The arms continually move in circles so that no movement in itself is complete but is always working to-

wards its opposite end, and as in the Kung Fu circle, there is no end, but only the beginning of another movement.

Also to be considered is the health aspect of Kung Fu. The exercises involve every muscle and joint of the body, therefore, are physically invigorating and mentally tranquil. These exercises stress slow respiration, balanced relaxed postures, good even breathing. Hence, digestion as well as the function of the internal organs and blood circulation are enhanced.

The relationship of Yin and Yang and the five elements which sprang from their interaction also strongly influence the ideas fundamental to Chinese medicine. Acupuncture, which has so recently drawn the attention of the Western World, forms an important part of Chinese medicine. And Kung Fu, in conjunction with acupuncture plays a very important part in the Chinese program of preventive medicine, because it does improve circulation, tones the body and relaxes the nervous system.

Further, the principles of Yin and Yang are also incorporated into the form. Although in movement, Yin and Yang act independently, the two fuse into one in quietude. All the movements follow the yielding principles to react according to the bending and stretching movements of the opponent.

When the opponent's force is met with a soft retreat, it is called evasion. To follow a retreating opponent without losing touch is called adherence. Although there are myriads of variations to action and counteraction, the basic principles are the same.

Legend has it that in the sixth century A.D., Bodhidharma called Tamo, traveled from India to China to spread his teachings of Buddhism. He noticed, that during his lectures to the monks, they often fell asleep because of their poor physical condition. He therefore, introduced his exercises of sinew change to improve their health and assist their meditation. The emphasis was on rhythmic breathing, bending and stretching.

As the monks in the Shaolin temple were in constant physical danger, and were, by their religious code, forbidden to bear weapons, they combined these exercises with their philosophical principles and developed a highly sophisticated form of weaponless defense, based on a smooth flow of action, proper breathing and the utilization of an inner power called ch'i.

And so arose the foundation for the form of self defense completely contradictory to previous styles. Up to now the martial arts recognized only speed and strength, based on the false assumption that moving faster and faster developed proficiency. Instead, the new breed of fighters were trained to relax completely, avoid the use of muscular force, and yield before the opponent. In other words, when he meets an opponent, he neither resists nor counters the blow, but rather he yields before the blow, thus taking advantage of his opponent's momentum and adds a push or pull so that with the augmented impetus, the opponent meeting no resistance is thrown to the ground. That is how a mere four ounces can topple a thousand pounds. The four ounces do not defeat the thousand pounds, but rather helps the stronger force defeat itself. This action exemplifies the concept of "giving up oneself and yielding before the opponent." Also, although speed is the final objective, the training of the true artist involves the practice of slowness of movement so that he develops an inner sensitivity.

Finally, true Kung Fu involves harmonious, balanced, physical movements which blend with the mind. Coupled with deep rhythmical breathing, there is produced bodily and spiritual freedom and calmness of mind.

Kung Fu is not based on speed and strength which are natural abilities, but rather on study, practice and learning. Kung Fu is art ... Kung Fu is health ... Kung Fu is self-defense.

Styles of Kung Fu

Unfortunately there is no way of knowing how many styles and systems of Kung Fu have existed since its inception. Due to lack of records, the esoteric nature of the art, and the transmutation of styles, much has been lost to history. Of the styles that exist today, there are thousands; many of which are slight modifications of each other. In general they cover a broad area of martial arts which include empty hand fighting, weaponry, warfare and military strategy. The most numerous variations occur in the empty hand fighting. This art is broken into two main classifications; the hard style and the soft style . . . and these are subdivided into an endless number of styles based on different philosophies and movements . . . especially the movements of animals, insects and birds.

It is generally acknowledged that most styles are direct offshoots of the Five Formed Fist style which is basically an imitation of animal movements.

The multiplicity of styles increased as new information was added to the melting pot. More often than not as a teacher perfected a style, he added movements of his liking and deleted incompatible movements and so was born a new style bearing his name. In other cases two or more styles were combined to give rise to still another variety. Generally, it was necessary for a true master to learn many styles, because when he was challenged it was necessary for him to defend himself against any style or against any weapon.

There is also a multitude of weapons forms, most of which are a layover from military techniques, such

7

as the sword, spear, saber, bow and arrow. Individual countries formulated their own weapons which increased the pool of systems such as the Ninjutsu of Japan.

Other weapons styles were an innovation of necessity. Ancient China was inundated with roadside bandits and when under attack, one had to improvise in order to survive. A favorite weapon became the staff. The staff was used for walking, and also to carry burdens. If one were attacked the walking stick became a weapon, and if there was a pot on either end, he merely had to slip it off and had a ready means of repelling bandits.

Also out of necessity arose other less conventional weapons. For the most part these weapons were a creation of farmers and natives of occupied lands. Generally, under occupation laws, weapons of any kind were forbidden. Many of these ingenious people designed weapons out of farm implements or other innocent appearing artifacts. Thus arose the weapons styles of the scythe, the sickle, the non-chakus which were grain beaters on the farms of Okinawa, and the pitchfork, to name a few.

In the second century, Hua To, a famous surgeon designed a series of exercises for purposes of health and hygiene. These movements eventually infiltrated into the martial arts. They were fashioned after the tiger, deer, bear, monkey and bird.

A revolutionary development in the martial arts occurred in the thirteenth century. Chang Sen-feng, a Taoist monk, after watching a snake and crane battling, observed the value of yielding to the force of strength, and also the value of continuity of movement and so was added to the previous hard style of Kung Fu, the principle of softness and yielding.

Most of the empty hand movements were an emulation of animal movements. In ancient times, the masters would sit out in the forests and observe these motions, noting that each species defended itself in a manner which coincided with its anatomy. From the tiger, he observed speed, strength, agility, and the clawing motions. From the Crane, he learned grace. From the monkey he learned feigning, balance and swing arm movements.

A major development occurred during the sixteenth century. A young fighter, Kwok Yuen, who had practiced at the Shaolin Temple, expanded Tamo's eighteen exercises into seventy-two. An expert in the martial arts, he felt that Shaolin fighting was not a complete system and so he set out for distant lands in the hope of acquiring the knowledge needed to perfect the existing system. On his journey, he met Pak Yook Fong, a boxing master, and an old man known as Li. After an exchange of ideas and techniques, the three returned to the Shaolin Temple and increased the existing seventy-two exercises into one hundred and seventy, and classified them into five distinct styles, patterned after the motions of animals. These were:

> Tiger form . . . represents bone development and strength
> Crane form . . . represents sinew training and spiritual development
> Dragon form . . . represents inner movements rather than external
> Leopard form . . . represents swiftness and agility
> Snake form . . . represents inner strength of ch'i

It was these three men who laid the foundation for a new and effective style from which the Five Form Fist developed, and it is from this style that most other systems evolved.

Besides these "pure" styles, there were also a number of systems developed from combining one or more styles. For example, in Southern China, there is a style called Hung gar Kung Fu. It traces back to the animal forms of the Shaolin Temple and is more popularly known as the tiger-crane style. According to legend, a famous monk of the Shaolin Temple, a master of the tiger-claw tactics was walking through the temple garden. Suddenly a huge white crane swooped down and started picking on the vegetables. He picked up a stick and swung at the crane. The crane slowly raised one leg to avoid the strike. Then as the monk charged forward, the crane, with his large wings, swept himself backwards gracefully. Try as he may the monk could not affect a blow on the agile, fluid elusive crane. Upon returning to his room, he thought about the encounter with the crane and systematized a series of smooth, graceful movements corresponding to the movements of the crane. He combined these with his tiger crane technique to form the tiger-crane style.

One last style which emulates the movements of a monkey swinging from tree to tree was the Choy Li Fut Pai, named after two monks who developed the style. During the Ching Dynasty, the revolutionaries, who were not true fighters, were taught a very effective and aggressive style, that could be learned quickly. The movements were strange, beautiful, sweeping gestures, in which the arms move in a circular fashion like a rotating windmill. Often these fighters would yell battle cries, which are used in many styles today to unnerve the opponent. At that time, however the cries had a different meaning. They were used to identify the revolutionaries to each other.

Listed below are a few of the Kung Fu styles still in existence:

        Shaolin. . . . tiger
        Ch'uan-shu . . bear
        Pa-Kua . . . . . monkey
        Chiao-ti----bird
        Hua-Chuan---leopard
        Shou-pu . . . . . dragon
        Hung . . . . . crane
        Fut
        Hung Put Pai
        Li
        Choy Li Fut Pai
        Tai Chi Chuan
        Tong Long Pai
        Bak Hok Pai

Geographically, styles are also divided into Northern and Southern Styles. Some of those indigenous to the north are the Wing Chun, Pa-Kua, Northern Preying Mantis, Eagle Claw, Tan Tui, Ying yee and the Northern Monkey Styles. In the South there is the Southern Preying Mantis, Dragon Style, White Crane, Choy Lay Fut, Hung Gar, and Mot Gar.

In concluding this section, let me state that no style is better than any other. Like all techniques and philosophies, what works well for one man, may result in dismal failure in the hands of another. There are a multitude of reasons why one style becomes prominent, while another fades away into obscurity. Many men cultivate fighting as an art while others cultivate it for effectiveness. And so, reasons for style development become as countless as the number of people involved. But in the final analysis, it is the development and propagation of the art as a whole, that makes Kung Fu the beautiful entity that it is.

The Great PHILOSOPHERS and their PHILOSOPHIES

"Is not all philosophy a journey whose importance lies not in the end of the journey, but rather in the multitude of experiences met along the way."

Kung Fu was derived not from one man or one philosophy or any other singular force . . . but rather from a myriad of forces. Some of the more obvious influences which molded the art form are the many superstitions existing at the time of its inception, the religious thinkers who added much substance to its foundation, the socio-political forces which demanded conformity or non-conformity, the many purposes for which one develops such an art, and finally the philosophies of the ancients which still exert their influence on the world today.

It is the latter consideration that I will first discuss. First of all, I feel that no art, profession, or ideology could undergo purposeful evolution, without a strong philosophical foundation. Also, accomplishment and proficiency in any art is almost impossible without a firm knowledge of its connected history and philosophy. It is the purpose of this section not only to present the philosophical evolution, but also to acquaint the reader with the terminology and vocabulary needed to better understand Kung Fu not only as a system of self defense, but also as a reservoir of deep and valuable philosophical principles.

And so let us begin . . . .

All phases of life have symbolic representation.

The eagle is symbolic of our great country; Russia is represented by a hammer and cycle; in professions, a balance indicates the legal system, while the symbol of medicine is caduceus; in athletics, animals are the chosen representatives of most teams . . . so forth and so on. So too with the art of Kung Fu. There are two symbols which represent the art . . . the double fish configuration and the spiral configuration:

SPIRAL ....

DOUBLE FISH ....

These figures are symbolic of the art form Kung Fu.

Both these figures are symbolic of the art form Kung Fu and both have similar interpretations. Following is a brief history of the evolution of these symbols and interpretation of their meaning and their relationship to the art.

During the Sung Dynasty, about 1000 A.D., Chou Tung, a metaphysician, observed that nature exists in series of cyclical orderliness . . . i.e., everything known to man is born, evolves, dies, and is born again thus returning to the never ending circle . . . in effect with no beginning or end. This process is easily noticed in the changing seasons as Spring slowly but purposely changes into Summer; then Summer fading into Autumn; Autumn with its beautifully changing colors turns into Winter; and finally Winter melting away into Spring, thus completing the circle.

We see this same cyclical phenomenon in the transmutation of day into night. As the brilliance of the sun fades below the horizon, twilight covers the earth and then unnoticeably turns into nighttime. . . . then the sun returns, bringing with it the new daylight. Even the sun, the earth and all the planets themselves owe their existence to cyclical patterns.

Finally, the most dramatic example of cyclical existance is man himself, who is born into this world as a babe, evolves into manhood, gracefully enters old age and finally passes away . . . then according to the Buddhistic teachings of reincarnation, returns again to continue this cyclical evolution.

Is it not a known physical principal, developed by learned scientists, that matter can neither be created or destroyed? Why then should this same principle seem foreign to us?

Not only did Chou Tung observe the cyclical relationship of things, but also that this existence is dependent upon the transmutation of two opposite attributes which were assigned the comprehensive terms of yin and yang. In other words, the transformation of one opposite state of existence into another opposite is a slow methodical, predictable change. . . . or as Chou Tung states . . . a transmutation. Night does not immediately change into its opposite attribute, day. But rather this change is a smooth, effortless, transformation which is hardly noticeable and yet the change is so complete as to be noticeable . . . so that the end result is a complete transmutation.

And finally he states not only do these opposite attributes exist in harmony with each other, and complement each other, but also are interdependent. How can one appreciate the beauty and serenity of winter's snow unless one has the reference of a hot smoldering summer? How can one appreciate the warmth of a summer day, without experiencing the cold of a freezing winter? How can one enjoy the relaxation of a weekend without reference to a busy, hectic work-filled week? How can one enjoy returning to work unless one is bored with the relaxation of a weekend? And so everything behaves as a complement to its opposite, so that not only is there an existing harmony between all things in life but also there exists a complementary and interdependent relationship.

In short, Chou Tung observed and recorded, that all things in nature are cyclical, and this behavior is dependent on the transmutation of two opposite attributes, which exist in harmony, compliment each other and are dependent on each other?

Evolution of Kung Fu symbol

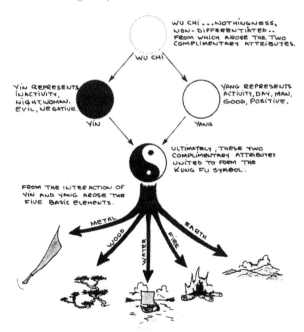

From these observations, he designed the Kung Fu double fish configuration to represent these characteristics.

Spiral. . . .

Summarizing, the circle is indicative of the cyclical evolution in nature. The transmutation of two opposites is represented by the dark area blending into the white. Harmony between these oppoite attributes is shown by the equality of the two areas. Finally the white dot in the dark area and the dark dot in the white area show the interdependency of the two. Obviously these same principles are applicable to the spiral configuration, however, its origin is not as clear.

The origin of the spiral configuration is indeed obscure. It is generally believed, however, that it did exist before the doublefish diagram, and was derived from the I-Ching, the Chines philosophy

Double Fish. . . .

of Change, and became symbolic of the martial arts and the philosophy of Kung Fu. During the evolution of the art, the spiral configuration was adopted by the intellectuals and scholars. . . . and the double fish configuration became associated with the common people.

In any case, both these diagrams became symbolic of the philosophy of Kung Fu as well as the martial art aspect. The analogy between the diagrams and the art is as a long flowing river, whose waters run smoothly and endlessly. All the movements in Kung Fu are circular, therefore endless . . . no beginning, no end. These movements can neither increase or diminish in size, like the constant flow of the stream. Finally everything that is, eventually passes away, only to return again.

The relationship between the symbols and the martial arts is best expressed by Chang Sang-feng, a Taoist priest of the thirteenth century who in his treatise on Kung Fu stated:

"In any motion, the whole body should move lightly and nimbly and it is especially important that all parts of the body must string together to complete coordination and balance."

"In any movement and in any part of the body, the two complementary aspects, substantial and insubstantial should be clearly differentiated and in each movement there is always a substantial as well as an insubstantial aspect of its own."

"In movement, the Yin and Yang act independently; in quietude, the two fuse into one. There should be no exceeding or falling short. All the movements follow the yielding principle to react according to the bending and stretching movements of the opponent."

"When your opponent brings pressure on your left side, you respond by allowing your left side to be empty. When your opponent brings pressure on your right side, you respond by allowing your right side to be empty. The more your opponent pushes upward or downward against you, the more he should feel there is no limit to the emptiness he encounters."

"In Kung Fu, the Yin cannot be separated from its complimentary part the Yang, and likewise the Yang cannot be separated from its complementary part the Yin. It is only when the Yin and the Yang interplay harmoniously in their proper relationship, that there is strength."

"It must be remembered that whenever one part of the body moves, all parts of the body move; when one part of the body comes to a standstill, the rest of the body follows."

"All movement should be like reeling silk from a cocoon. . . . it must be done smoothly and evenly without interruption, or breakage will occur . . . an interruption which could be utilized by an opponent."

In conclusion, the movements of Kung Fu, like the flowing lines of the diagram, involve the movements of the whole body, in unison . . . one piece . . . without interruption, as though all the movements are one. Such gracefulness in movement is the result of an imaginary linkage. These uninterrupted and coordinated movements represent the highest form of Kung Fu technique and are the ultimate towards which every student should aim.

the Great Philosophers

Kung Fu is unique and separate from most other martial arts in that it represents a profound physical and psychological manifestation of ancient philosophy, which has evolved over several thousand years of Chinese civilization. This philosophy is an amalgamation of ancient superstition, socio-political

Life itself is an endless cycle of change—like the seasons: Summer, Fall, Winter, Spring.

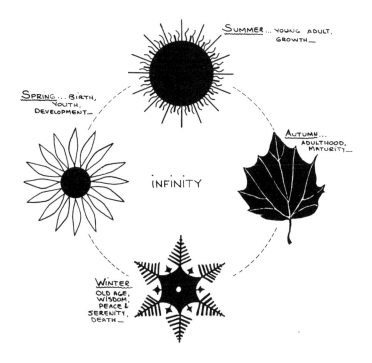

SUMMER... YOUNG ADULT, GROWTH—

SPRING... BIRTH, YOUTH, DEVELOPMENT—

AUTUMN... ADULTHOOD, MATURITY—

INFINITY

WINTER OLD AGE, WISDOM, PEACE L SERENITY, DEATH—

pressures and most of all the contributions of three great men; namely, Lao Tzu, Confucius, and Buddha.

In order to better understand the art for the beautiful entity that it is, an aquaintance with these men and their teachings will give us a greater perspective. Oddly enough, these sages lived at approximately the same time, and their influence on the lives of thousands of people has been unparalleled throughout history.

Lao Tzu and Taoism

Lao Tzu, the Chinese sage, taught to his disciples the doctrine of the Tao. According to history, he was born in Ch'u in Honan province c. 604 B.C. Little is known of his earlier life, except that he worked at the imperial palace as custodian of the imperial archives. Like most of the people of his time he was distraught over the existing political tyranny, and finally at the age of 160, he decided to withdraw from the unbearable way of life under the Chou dynasty. He left the Middle Kingdom on a wagon which was drawn by a black ox and rode away. As he reached the Han-Ku pass, the gatekeeper, Yin-Hsi asked him to leave a record of his teachings. Lao Tzu compiled his teachings in a manuscript consisting of 5,280 words. This writing was called the Tao Te Ching and was to have a profound effect on the Chinese mind.

It is the Tao which so greatly influences our art of Kung Fu. All the precepts of the Tao can be defined in each and every movement of the art. And the philosophy of Lao Tzu as well as the philosophy of Kung Fu are one.

The Tao te Ching, is a compilation of Lao Tzu's teachings. Etymologically, Tao refers to the way or the path that one should follow; te refers to virtue or power; Ching is a book or a classic. Hence, Tao te Ching means the Classic of the Way and the Power.

The doctrine of the Tao is one of naturalism i.e., eternal life and/or salvation is not to be found in the striving, aggressive ways of the world; nor is salvation to be found on the level of magic incantations as prayer or invocations, nor is it to be found on the basis of liturgical ritual indigenous to so many religions throughout the world. Lao Tzu taught that the only means of attaining a full life, blessed with serenity and peace with one's self is through the observation of nature and living in accordance with the ways of nature. Nothing should be done contrary to the natural way. . . . we should bend with the wind, so to speak, and in this way become a part of it, rather than attempt to resist. A leaf covered with snow does not resist, but merely bends slowly, gracefully, and finally the snow falls away . . . no resistance, no effort, but rather a yielding, a giving of itself to the stress of the snow and finally victory.

All life should be as the blade of grass in the wind. . . . as the snow covered leaf. . . . effortless, smooth, natural. The way of nature, therefore, becomes the ultimate reality . . . it gives birth to, regulates, and ultimately terminates all things.

Coinciding with this doctrine of naturalism, Lau Tzu spoke of two complementary principles which not only complement the philosophy of naturalism, but reinforce it.

The doctrine of the "Uncarved Block" represents the second part of the trilogy. It depicts man in his virgin state of existence; unspoiled by the pressures of society, unaltered by the bigotry of education, untouched by the greed of economics.

It is a known fact that man is a conditioned animal. Conditioned by the pressures of family, education, and finally social standards. He is constantly bombarded by his environmental background. He is born into this world, raised in a proper neighborhood, attends proper schools, becomes a member of a proper church, enters his proper place in society, so forth and so on. And yet, how influential are the schools, churches, and society in molding his thinking so that his thoughts are not his own, but rather the thoughts and ideas and even the words of the people and institutions with which he has associated? Generally, people are Catholic or Protestants because they were born into the particular faith; they enter certain specified colleges through the coercion of their parents or friends; they speak and behave in the manner dictated by the people of the circle in which they live.

Lao Tzu holds that this conditioned animal is contrary to what nature had intended . . . indeed, man is no longer man but a conditioned animal that responds to stimuli in a prescribed manner. Man, to be true man, must elevate himself to the level on which he belongs, that of a rational creature. He must return to the original state of his existence . . . the uncarved block . . . and fill his mind and heart with those things that are fitting and proper and in keeping with the natural laws. By so doing, he will be fulfilled . . . he will be at peace with himself . . . he will be complete.

The third major principle of which Lao speaks is the doctrine of "Wu Wei" . . . or non-action. Non-action does not imply doing nothing, or an extension of the doctrine of turning one's cheek; but rather taking only that action which is in accord with the natural law. This principle was difficult for most of the people to understand, especially during the political turmoil of that time. When persecutions were rampant, and imprisonment so prevalent, a policy of non-action was difficult to comprehend. However, Lao Tzu was trying to tell them that force against force was a futile approach to the problems of the day, particularly against the strength of the militaristic government. It would be better, he said, to yield to strength, and in this way imbalance the opponent and in effect give the balance of power to the people . . . . a difficult philosophy for the majority of the peasants.

Because of the depth of Lao Tzu's doctrines, the

masses, who were mainly illiterate were incapable of comprehending his teachings. As a result, the popularity of Taoism took much time to mature. And yet his thoughts were not indigenous to the Chinese mind, for 600 years later, a man gave rise to a religion which swept the world . . . based on the same doctrines as those spoken by Lao Tzu. Note, if you will not only the similarity of ideas, but even the words in the following quotations;

New Testament
Be good to those who hate
   you . . . Luke 6:27

He who lives by the sword,
      shall die by the sword . . . Mat. 26:52

Behold the lamb of God who
      bears the sins of the
      world . . . John 1:29

For he who would be first,
      finds himself last; and
   the last shall be first . . . Mk 9:35

What profits a man if he gains
      the whole world, yet loses
         his soul . . . Mat 16:26

Ask and ye shall receive; seek
   and ye shall find Matt 7:7

Except ye become as little
   children, ye shall not enter
      the kingdom of God . . . Mat. 18:3

Tao Te Ching
Requite hatred with virtue
    a violent man dies a violent
            death.
who bears himself the sins of
    the world, is the king of
            the world,
    the sage puts himself last and
        finds himself in the foremost
                place.
One's own self or material
    goods, which has more worth

Work it and more comes out;
    draw upon it as you will,
        it never runs dry.
In controlling your vital force,
        and to achieve gentleness,
    can you become as the
            newborn child.

Confucius

The second great sage who contributed so much to the evolution of Chinese philosophy was Confucius (551-479 B.C.). His family name was K'ung Ch'iu, which became latinized to K'ung Fu-tzu. He was born of a noble family in the state of Lu in modern Shantung. His father died when Confucius was three years old and the family became very poor. As a result of this he became a self-educated man. In spite of this he dedicated his life to teaching and became the first person in Chinese history to dedicate his life to eliminate illiteracy. His purpose in education, however, was not the formal instruction with which we are familiar but rather to teach man how to live with man, or rather a standard of propriety and behavior.

At age 51, he became the minister of justice in Lu. His attempts to recruit the help of his superiors in propagating his doctrine was met with disdain, and so he started a 13 year ministry, in an attempt to disseminate his political, social and philosophical beliefs, taking with him many of his pupil-apostles. Finally, he returned, unsuccessfully, at the age of 68 to write the impact his teachings would have on Chinese culture.

Unfortunately, there is little, if any proof of his having met with Lao Tzu. Also little verification exists as to whether or not he wrote the ancient classics such as the Spring and Autumn Annals, the Book of Changes or the I-Ching, and the Analects, and controversy as to the authorship of these great works survives even today.

As Taoism was a philosophy of naturalism, Confucius advocated a philosophy of humanism. He did not concern himself with the after-world or other spiritual considerations. His doctrine was directed towards the world of the living and from this attitude evolved extreme and elaborate codes of conduct and rapport which in effect controlled man's social behavior. Specifically, his code related:

1. virture and morality in government
2. righteousness in morality
3. filial piety in families
4. proper conduct in social situations

Therefore, Confucianism was worldly and conforming. . . . it was humanistic and concerned itself with social order; Taoism, on the contrary was transcendental and non-conforming . . . it was naturalistic and not at all concerned with social order, but rather the order of life of the individual.

However Confucianism had a greater appeal to the masses than did Taoism for three reasons. In China the majority of people were illiterate, and those who could read were incapable of understanding the meaning of Lao Tzu's teachings. Confucianism, on the other hand was a rather simple easily understood and practical way of life. Secondly, Taoism had the flavor of submissiveness and was almost feminine in character, whereas Confucianism spoke of chivalry and codes of conduct, and so related more closely to manhood. Finally most of the people were orientated towards religious incantations and ritual for their salvation and so it was simple to replace old habits and words with newer and simpler ones.

Buddhism

The third corner of our trilogy of great sages is Buddha. He was an Indian prince, born c. 506 B.C. He was a very rich and pampered youth, who spent his days in the grandeur of the courtyards enjoying all the fineries of life afforded by a young prince. He was unaware of the struggle for life that existed beyond the palace walls . . . ignorance, malnutrition, sickness, and the daily depravations suffered by the people. One day he ventured into the city and was shocked at the sight of suffering and death that filled his kingdom. He saw hoards of people starving, begging for food, and dead or near dead bodies strewn along the streets. He was unable to accept what he saw as real. From this experience, he formed the basis of his teachings, that everything is an illusion . . . nothing is real.

Buddha proposed a doctrine of disregard of self and materialism and emphasized the next life and the world beyond. Needless to say, the appeal of this new religion was accepted with great zeal. In a country where the majority looked at life as a wretched existence at best, and the possibility to improve their lot was non-existent, the promise of a happy life beyond the grave, gave hope and purpose to the multitudes.

He preached that man's suffering results from his attachment to material things, because material things do not exist, they are illusionary. . . . therefore when they pass away, man becomes distraught and frustrated. And so, man must free himself from this attachment to materialism and achieve the state referred to as "nirvana." And now, he must abandon the final illusion . . . the realization that the ego . . . the self is real. From these observations, he formulated the following hypothesis:

1. existence is suffering
2. People are repeatedly born to lead many lives
3. the soul is able to find eternal peace only by extinguishing the ego or the self.

Unlike the humanistic code of Confucianism which regulated man's relationship to man and a proper code of conduct, or the nature worship of Taoism and the appeal to a soft, yielding way of life, this new religion was concerned with the after life and chartered a route to the world beyond the grave.

"The Four Basic Truths of Buddhism," from the foundation of his teachings and are the basis from which the sophistication of Buddhism grew:

1. There does exist suffering . . . all existence, all life, is an endless cycle of pain, sufferring and unhappiness . . . birth, aging and finally death.
2. Existence and ignorance are the causes of suffering. . . . the ego alone is the cause of all illusion and so of all evil.
3. Possibility of being liberated from suffering . . . . we can only be free when we free ourselves from material attachment and finally . . . free ourselves from the illusion of self.

4. The path which is to be followed.

Eventually, Buddhism branched into two main schools of thought . . . the Hinayana, or ancient school of wisdom which was an extremely rigid form of Buddhism based on the old texts and rituals; and the Mahayana or new school of wisdom which offered more flexibility and adaptability, and tended to disregard ancient teachings. Both these schools were concerned with the same end, the attainment of spiritual illumination, but like most other religions advocated different paths.

Of importance to our essay is the development of Zen (Japanese) or Ch'an (Chinese) as an offshoot of the Mahayan branch of Buddhism coupled with the Taoist influence.

Buddism ⟨ Hinayana branch / Mahayan branch

Taoism ⟶ Ch'an or Zen

Buddhism was introduced into China by an Indian monk, Bodhidharma c. 500 A.D. Ch'an or Zen was a revolution of Buddhism in China in an effort to separate the Indian mind from the Chinese. And once again there was a schism of Ch'an, dividing it into a Northern School of gradual enlightenment and a Southern School of sudden enlightenment. Eventually Ch'an spread into Japan and was called Zen, and since its inception has grown to become the foremost religious philosophy in the country.

Summarizing, there are three doctrines of Eastern philosophy which have greatly influenced the Eastern world as well as been instrumental in the evolution of the art of Kung Fu, thus affecting the physical and mental aspects, both of which are combined to form the complete and perfect art. The doctrines are:

1. Confucianism . . . a doctrine of humanism, based on the efficacy of ritual and conformity as the means to salvation.
2. Taoism . . . a doctrine of naturalism based on the soft, yielding, ways of nature.
3. Buddhism . . . a doctrine of non-materialism based on the realization that all is illusionary.

The Triology of Philosophies

BUDDHA

LAO TZU

CONFUCIUS

In concluding this section, the three great sages and their tremendous impact on the Eastern mind, and especially their influence in the evolution of

Kung Fu, I would like to leave you with these few thoughts. It is not difficult to see how directly the principles of Taoism are intertwined in the philosophy of Kung Fu. . . . particularly the doctrines of inner calmness, softness, yielding, non-action, naturalism etc. Confucianism as well as Buddhism also share in the formation of Kung Fu as the total martial art. . . . their obvious contributions include proper breathing, hygiene, ch'i, inner strength, as well as proper respect for man and his emotions, a better understanding of life and its relationship to everything else . . . and finally the importance of proper living and a total perspective of the divine plan as seen through the eyes of the Eastern world. So great an impact did these philosophies have on the Chinese, that the concept of Zen as a result of the contributions of Buddhism, Confucianism, and Taoism, swept the whole continent and to this day, is one of the predominant philosophies . . . it has, in effect become a way of life for millions of people.

Other
Contributing Factors
affecting
The Evolution of Kung Fu

The School of Yin and Yang

The concept of Yin and Yang was an attempt by the ancients, to create some degree of harmony and purpose to the pre-existing chaotic concepts of cosmology. It was the intent of the ancients to reduce the universe and all its activities to a geometric equation, thus creating a purposeful relationship between cause and effect. They were able to do this by utilizing the Yin and Yang concept along with the philosophy set forth by the I-Ching.

In its simplest form the doctrine of Yin and Yang teaches that all occurrences, all happenings, every action and reaction is the result of two elements, forces or principles; yin, which is negative, passive, and weak . . . . and Yang, which is positive, active and strong. Out of the interaction of these two opposites, arose the five agents . . . metal, wood, water, fire, and earth, which add the important concept of cyclical activity (the I-Ching or Book of Change) . . . . in which things succeed each other as the five agents take successive turns.

Therefore, the universe becomes an orderly state of existence involving a continuous change, in which all things are interfused and intermingled in a cyclical transmutation. And now we have a natural operations

31

of forces which can be determined and predicted objectively. Everything became personalized or was assigned a number to reduce existence to the simplest formula. Out of this organized relationship arose codes of conduct for society, morality, systems, and cultures, because the end result of this theory of interaction was predictable. Through their interaction arose the five elements which are the first of nine categories. Some of the other categories are listed below as a point of interest.

1st Category . . . the Five Agents
  Water . . . moistens and descends . . . . .
    therefore produces softness
  Fire . . . . burns and ascends . . . .
    therefore produces bitterness
  Wood . . . . is crooked and straight . . .
    therefore produces sourness
  Metal . . . yields and is modified . . . .
    therefore produces acridity
  Earth . . . is sowed and reaped . . . .
    therefore produces sweetness
2nd Category . . . the Five Activities
  Appearance . . virtue is respectfulness . . .
    leads to gravity
  Speech . . . . . . virtue is reasoning . . . .
    leads to orderliness
  Seeing . . . . . . virtue is clearness . . . .
    leads to wisdom
  Hearing . . . . . virtue is distinctness . . . . .
    leads to deliberation
  Thinking . . . . virtue is depth . . . . .
    leads to sageness.
4th Category . . . the Five Arrangements of Time
  The Year
  The Day

The Stars, planets and Zodiacal Signs
The Month
The Calendaric Calculations
9th Category . . . The Five Blessings
Longevity
Wealth
Physical and Mental health
Love of Virtue
An End Crowning Life.
Other Correlations of the Five Agents:
5 directions
5 grains
5 virtues
5 musical notes
5 senses
5 ancient empires
5 colors
5 metals
5 atmospheric condition

Each of the five agents is related to the other categories . . . if wood is a sign given by heaven, for example in the form of a tree, then the corresponding color, direction etc., is chosen.

During the reign of the Yellow Emperor, a sign appeared to him in the form of earthworms and mole crickets. He said, "The force of Earth is Dominant," and so he chose yellow as his color and Earth as the model for his activities.

In the time of Yü, he observed that during the autumn and winter, the green grass and trees held their beauty. He accepted this as a sign, saying, "The force of Wood is dominant", and so he chose green as his color and wood as the model for his activities.

During the T'ang dynasty, metal blades appeared in the waters of the palace pool. T'ang recognized the

The five directions and their related signs.

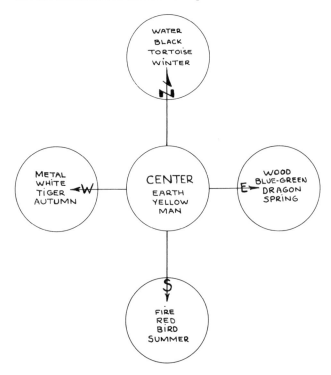

sign and said, "The force of Metal is dominant," and
he chose white as his color and Metal as the model for
his activities.

And so, in the Yin Yang School, the universe becomes a well coordinated system in which everything
is related, and for the ancients, this concept yielded a
degree of orderliness. By relying on these principles,
the people were able to plan their lives, present and
future, make decisions, pass judgement and in effect,
the lives of the ancients did indeed become a sophisti-

cated equation, in which, given the proper information on one side, they were able to successfully predict the outcome on the other. No aspect of Chinese civilization whether metaphysics, medicine, government, or art escaped its influence.

I-Ching . . . . the Book of Changes

The I-Ching is a clear outline of a rational approach to a well-ordered and dynamic universe as outlined by the ancients of China. It arose out of the ancient practice of divination and became a constant source of referral and prognostication. The name as well as the rationale refers to the constant change, based on the interaction of two complementary forces. The I-Ching is thought to be about 3000 years old, but has come to be timeless. Originally, it was a manual of oracles, and evolved into a book of wisdom, becoming one of the great Five Confucian Classics. It became a common source for both Confucian and Taoist philosophy. The central theme of the book, is constant change, and the transformation underlying all existence. Obviously this concept of constant change as well as the principles of Yin and Yang have both been incorporated as an integral part of Kung Fu.

According to legend, the system of the I-Ching was devised by Fu Hsi (2953-2838 B.C.), the first of the Five Legendary Emperors. While meditating in the forest one day, he observed a tortoise with strange markings on his back, from which he is said to have fashioned the eight diagrams which are the foundation of the I-Ching.

The Book consists of 64 Hexagrams, which are based on the 8 trigrams above. Each hexagram is followed by an explanation of the whole hexagram and then an explanation of the component lines.

Diagram of 64 Hexagrams shown in a circle and in a square, based on Fu Hsi's 8 trigrams

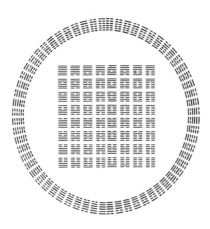

The I-Ching is based on the 64 hexagrams which represents all possible situations, probabilities and institutions. Each of the above hexagrams is followed by an explanation of the whole hexagram and then by an explanation of each component line.

The oracles of ancient China were able to foretell one's future by constructing a hexagram for each individual and then interpreting this hexagram. Initially yarrow sticks were used. They were cut from yarrow stalks and trimmed to the same length. Fifty of these yarrow sticks were used and through a succession of throws, the hexagram was designed. With the introduction of

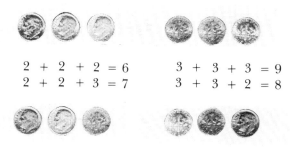

$$2 + 2 + 2 = 6 \qquad 3 + 3 + 3 = 9$$
$$2 + 2 + 3 = 7 \qquad 3 + 3 + 2 = 8$$

bronze coins in China, this tedious procedure was discarded and the throwing of three coins at a time was substituted. Each side of the coin was assigned a value . . . heads a value of 2; tails a value of three. They were thrown six times, one for each line of the hexagram, and were designed from the bottom up.

$$6 = -\ - \quad 7 = — \quad 8 = -\ - \quad 9 = —$$

For example; 1st throw = ——— 4th throw = ———
2nd throw = — 5th throw = ———
3rd throw = ——— 6th throw = —

then this particular hexagram would appear — Hence, the I-Ching and the Yin and Yang concept became a basis for prognostication. The five activities and their interplay in all matters plus the Yin Yang concept became a guide for all aspects of society, morality, law, government, culture, etc.

The Subject of Ch'i

According to the ancient Chinese, the universe, man and nature are affected by three cosmic forces. . . . Yin and Yang and the five activities, the I-Ching or Book of Changes and Ch'i. They strongly believed that through a knowledge of these forces and the proper interpretation of the signs, all situations could be reduced to a simple formula from which action and result could be objectively determined and predicted.

It is a simple matter to see the relationship of the three forces to the martial arts and the philosophy underlying them. I would now like to discuss the most important and profound force, its relationship to the Chinese Culture, and most important its relationship to the martial arts. . . . the subject of Ch'i.

It is impossible to adequately define a term as nebulous and yet as profound as ch'i. It has been defined in thousands of ways by thousands of people. The ancients believed the activity of ch'i as the force responsible for the creation of the universe; all things, all people are born of, live dependent on, and die due to a lack of ch'i. An imbalance of this force resulted in catastrophe in the universe or sickness in the individual. Further they believed ch'i to be an energy which permeated the earth through a crisscross of divided pipelines, which carried a bewildering variety of vapors or invisible fluids from one place to another, and that these vapors controlled the balance of nature in the world, being responsible for such things as the seasons and the weather. Any imbalance in the vapors resulted in catastrophies to plague the universe as plague and famine. The ch'i of the universe is an ever present force, which has no beginning or end. . . . it neither increases nor diminishes, although it appears to change, it is nevertheless, changeless. Ultimately, everything that is. . . . the sun, the moon, the stars, you, I, the whole universe and everything in it is derived from ch'i.

Philosophically speaking, a neoteric definition of ch'i is less dogmatic than that proposed by the ancient Chinese. It has been defined as intrinsic energy, psychophysiological power, biophysical energy, vital force, activating force, matter-energy, material-spiritual force, so forth and so on. There is no word or group of words that can define ch'i in absolute terms. Like electricity, we know how to produce it, how to store it, how to use it, and we are able to see its effect. Suffice it to say ch'i is an intangible power associated with rhythmical respiration, stored in an imaginary area, the tan tien, which is defined as a hypothetical spot three inches below the navel. It is activated and directed by the mind and it is responsible for the movements of the body. Beyond these ambiguous definitions, what is known about ch'i is mostly a carryover from the ancient schools of hygiene, health culture, and martial arts.

In order for ch'i to be effective, it must first be cultivated, and secondly it must be exercised, so that the body and mind become one with the universe. Cultivation of ch'i is best accomplished by concentrating on a series of exercises involving rhythmical breathing. This conscious breathing, in which energy is held in balance inside the body, is aided by lowering the ch'i to the tan tien, thus lowering one's center of gravity thereby enhancing a more stable position. At this point, the mind and body become peaceful and tranquil, and all movements become graceful and harmonious. Breathing itself must be from the diaphragm, rather than the upper body which tends to upset one's stability. The mind as well as every bone and muscle in the body, becomes open thus allowing the ch'i to travel unobstructed.

In this relaxed and tranquil state the ch'i, through an act of the mind, is able to be channeled to one or all parts of the body in an instant, so that the entire body acts as one. . . . the mind controlling the ch'i, and the ch'i controlling the body.

Physiologically, I will define ch'i as it relates to the martial arts, i.e., as a unit of strength or power or dynamic energy rather than as a unit of health. Ch'i is looked at as a focusing of natural energy which can instantaneously be directed to any or all parts of the body. Everyone has ch'i power, however it is not developed to the same degree. Ch'i power is analagous to the powers of the subconscious mind. We all possess the faculty; we are all aware of its power. It is developed to different degrees in different people; and those who develop the faculty enjoy a high level of performance. The relationship of ch'i and the subconscious mind and their latent powers can be readily seen in the diagram of an iceberg, in which only 15% of the whole is perceived, whereas actually there is 85% below the water.
So too with ch'i. . . . those who do not develop this faculty are losing 85% of their strength.

Therefore, all true strength becomes a product of the ch'i rather than muscle. A fighter who has learned this secret and is able to calm his mind, lower his center of gravity, and make himself one with nature, strikes with the power of twenty men. . . . while the fighter of a lower level, using only muscle power strikes out aimlessly and ineffectively.

That ch'i is a property of all people is not hard to understand. This strange psychophysiologic

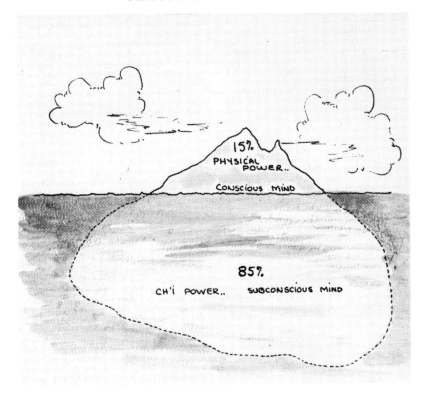

Ones capabilities and their utilization can be compared to the iceberg. Only 15% of the iceberg is realized because that is all that is seen above the water line. The major portion of this mass is unreckoned with—as are the latent powers of our subconscious mind.

phenomenon readily surfaces when needed and is unobstructed by conscious thought. We are all familiar with the story of the small, frail woman whose child was pinned under an automobile. She became so excited, she forgot her physical limitations, thereby inadvertently allowing her ch'i to circulate, and lifted the automobile unaided to save her daughter's life. Another case tells of a meek, moderately built man whose family was threatened by thieves and robbers. Without thinking, he became so impassioned at the thought of injury to his family, he attacked the thieves and even after being shot twice, fought on until the thieves disbanded and fled. A less dramatic story concerns an elderly Chinese couple, who everyday laid on their backs, breathed slowly and rhythmically, concentrating on an area three inches below their navels, and meditated. During this period, their graying heads turned to full thick crops of black hair. After their meditation, the gray color returned.

Only a very few of the martial arts masters have developed their ch'i to be able to perform "noi cun." In San Francisco, there is an elderly Chinese master who is capable of downing an opponent merely by pointing a finger.

What is the source of this power? What is its origin? Is it a faculty of the mind or the body or a combination of both. Many years ago, Alexander Graham Bell proposed his theory of ether which exists in the universe and in all men. It is through this ether that all men are related. Through this medium we are able to receive and transmit thought waves, suggestions and ideas. He also postulated that these waves are capable of exerting force which he attributed as the causative factor of psychokinesis. Today in modern psychology, this theory of thought transmission and psychokinesis has been used as a foundation in the research of positive mental attitude, telepathy, clairoyance, and extra-sensory-perception. Could it be that the ancient Chinese, years ago, formulated this same theory . . . . and only recently has the western world become aware of its existence?

If we accept the theory of psychokinesis, in which

one is capable of moving an object merely by thinking that it move . . . or according to Mr. Bell, if we send forth thought waves capable of exerting a force, and that this force is capable of moving an object. Also we must concede that this force may be augmented by many minds concentrating on the same result (effect of P.M.A. and group psychotherapy etc.). Hence, it is not too difficult to accept the theory of ch'i as being the same product of the mind. Like the increase in strength of a weight-lifter, who by daily practice is able to increase his power . . . why should we look askance at the ability of a man, who has trained and cultivated this power for years, who can drop an opponent merely by pointing a finger?

Ch'i is an intangible, it is an undefineable, it is ethereal. However, we do know it exists, we can see manifestations of its power. Very definitely this psychophysiological phenomenon is deeply rooted in Chinese philosophy and has become a very essential part of the philosophy as well as a very essential part of the martial arts itself.

The Great Literary Works

The development of Chinese philosophy and its effect on the martial arts would indeed be incomplete without at least a brief mention of the Great Literary Works of ancient Chinese culture. Suffice it to say that these classics did play an integral part as well as contribute to some degree to the martial arts. We will mention only those which are akin to our theme, and so give you some degree of familiarity with the literature of the times. The Confucian Classics and the Confucian Analects are by far the most influential literary works of ancient China.

I. The Confucian Classics . . . . these were the first five books of unknown authorship of ancient China. To this day there is an unending controversy as to whether or not Confucius wrote the Classics and the Analects. However they are called the Confucian Classics because supposedly his teaching are rooted in these books.

    A. The Book of Changes . . . I-Ching
        1. grew out of the ancient practice of divination, and was a rational approach to orderliness.
        2. The Ten Wings or Commentaries on the I-Ching . . . some ascribe to Confucius, others say it was the work of many hands from 5th century B.C. to 3rd century B.C.
    B. The Book of History . . . Shu Ching
        1. A collection of documents from the time of the legendary Emperor Yao (3rd millennium) to the early Chou Dynasty

C. The Book of Odes . . . Shih Ching
1. A collection of 305 poems including songs sung in religious and early official functions.
D. Spring and Autumn Annals
1. A collection of documents connected with the state of Lu, during the spring and autumn period 722-481 B.C.
E. The Book of Rites
1. Religiously orientated, honoring religious figures and related ceremonies

Initially there was a 6th classic, the Book of Music, however it has been lost.

II. Confucian Analects . . . . . This is the most authentic and reliable source of Confucian teachings. Consisted of his views on all aspects of life and standards of behavior as religion, rites and morals. It is unknown as to whether Confucius compiled this text, and like the classics, represents a point of endless controversy amongst scholars.

Chronological Evolution of Kung Fu

This chapter will be dedicated to the chronological Evolution of Kung Fu. Intertwined in its development, were the effects of great philosophers and their philosophies, the ancient Chinese culture and its concepts of religion, hygiene, and cosmology, and finally the effects of the politico-social turmoil that has racked China and continues to keep the country in the state of constant turbulence. I would like to develop this theme of chronology in conjunction with the politico-social events of the periods as they affected Kung Fu.

The art of fighting is as old as man himself, for man instinctively used his hands and feet for survival, to defend himself, and to defend his right to live as he chooses. With the passing of time, he developed weapons to increase his fighting ability such as clubs, spears and staffs, and so was born a system of self-defense. It was in China that fighting skills reached their zenith. China's preoccupation with health and longevity provided a foundation for the martial arts and contributed no small portion to its development. The impetus given the martial arts by monks, philosophers, scholars, and professional fighters made China a formidable military force. Unfortunately, due to its closed door policy to foreigners, it failed to develop the technological aspects. This coupled with a lack of good leadership has led to a drastic decline in the nation's military standing.

China's history of fighting is almost 5,000 years old as evidenced by wall paintings and murals in the tombs of the ancient emperors, as well as the excavated relics of that period. Historically, the first record of hygiene and fighting can be traced to the 3rd millennium B.C. to the period of the three Cultural Heroes or the Legendary Emperors of China. It is believed they developed and nationalized the art of medicine.

2873. . . . . Emperor Fu Hsia . . . instituted a form of medicine to be spread through China to maintain the health of his people.

2752. . . . . Emperor Shun Nung . . . contributed a classification of the herbs as an aid in healing.

2676. . . . . Emperor Huang-Ti . . . the legendary Yellow Emperor . . . he nationalized medicine by sending healers through the country to care for the health of his people. It was during his reign, that the first record of fighting appears. Chinese literature of this period refers to a very primitive form of wrestling called "Go-ti." Supposedly Go-ti originated from the legendary battle of Tuluk in which the Emperor Huang-ti overcame a horned monster called chi-yu. Go-ti became a form of competition and entertainment among the Emperor's warriors. The competitors wore two horns which were fastened to their heads and attempted to gore each other. The game became a favorite sport and spread throughout the land and was passed down through the generations. To this day, the dance is performed traditionally at art festivals in Honan and Manchuria. It is thought that the go-ti dance was adopted by the Japanese and with some alterations became their national sport of Sumo wrestling. It was exported to Japan during the Tang Dynasty (618-907 A.D.) and is the earliest known exportation of Kung Fu.

1111-249 B.C. . . . The Chou Dynasty

    a) The Book of Rites makes mention of the martial arts. Historians believe that during this period, the Taoist monks developed a series of health exercises based on health and meditation.

    b) The Spring and Autumn Annals and the Literature of the Warring States . . . Both of these works were written during this period and speak of archery, fencing and wrestling. Up to the period of the Warring States, the battlefield was a place for only nobility. However now, the commoner was allowed on this hallowed ground and the codes of chivalrous warfare gave ground to a more sanguinary character.

206 B.C.-220 A.D. . . . The Han Dynasty . . . during this period, Pan Kuo (32-92 A.D.) wrote his "HanSu I Wen Chih" or Han Book of the arts which contained four chapters on warfare and fighting. They were:

        1. Governmental Aspects of Occupation
        2. Battlefield Strategy
        3. Principles in Nature
        4. Fighting Skills . . . which included empty hand fighting arm and leg exercise, and the use of weapons.

In keeping with the principles set forth by Pan Kuo, there developed in China at this time, a form of empty hand fighting called "chi-chi." This was the transitional period of warfare where fighting had been a prerogative of nobility and now even the commoners fought . . . and they fought brilliantly. Concurrent with these developments was felt the impact of Lao Tzu (c.500 B.C.) and his doctrine of Taoism, the Tao te

Ching. In conjunction with his teachings and the doctrines of Buddha schools of health, hygiene, breath and meditation started flowering throughout China thus laying the foundation for Kung Fu.

During the closing years of the Han Dynasty, the first real contribution of worth was made to the annals of fighting, based on the works of a famous surgeon Dr. Hua To. He introduced a series of exercises based on the movements of animals which became the basis for many Kung Fu styles. He wrote in his book "Shou Pu", "the body needs exercise in order to promote free blood circulation and to prevent sickness, hence the practice of motion of the rotating bear's neck and the following animal movements of moving the joints to prevent old age. I have a system of exercises called the Frolic of the Five Animals. The movements of those of the tiger, deer, bear, monkey and the bird. This system removes disease, strengthens the legs and insures health. It promotes sweating and gives the feeling of lightness. It consists of jumping, twisting, swaying, crawling, rotating, and contracting."

Whether for fighting or for health the imitation of animals and birds played an important part in the evolution of Kung Fu, and the styles developed in the following manner:

Tiger form . . . bone development and dynamic strength

Crane form . . . sinew training and spiritual development

Dragon form . . inner strength rather than external

Leopard form . softness and agility

Snake form . . . inner strength or ch'i

The trend towards exercises and hygiene was augmented by the arrival in China of Buddhist monks, spreading the truth of Zen. The strongest influence as far as the martial arts are concerned was Bodhidaruma, called Tamo. In the 6th century he arrived at the Shaolin temple to teach Zen to the monks. Prior to this time, Kung Fu had been practiced only for self defense. However, it lacked the spiritual and meditative aspects that Zen was to contribute. Tamo introduced his sinew changing and marrow washing exercises to the poorly conditioned monks to keep them awake during his lectures. Eventually these exercises became a vital part of the internal system of Kung Fu.

Initially, Kung Fu was a closed institution and restricted to the monks because it was considered part of the religious unity of mind and body as practiced in Zen. Also because of the dangers of the art, they feared that the art would fall into the hands of evil people.

However, with the passage of time, merchants passing through the temple learned many of the techniques to defend themselves against the highway robbers, and so the secrets of the Shaolin temple started to trickle out. Later government persecutions and repeated burnings of the temple dispersed the monks who felt obliged to teach the art to the oppressed masses, so that they could defend themselves against corrupt government officials and bandits. And finally Kung Fu lost the religious flavor that had been such an important part of the system and became spread through China as a martial arts system only.

618-907 A.D. Tang Dynasty
960-1297 A.D. Sung Dynasty . . . this was the period

of China's Age of Chivalry. The heroics of the fighting monks added much impetus to the growing interest of Kung Fu. Also many contributions were made by the military to the art of fighting. One General Yueh Fei elaborated on the merit of Hsing-i. The flow of knowledge was no longer a trickle. The esoteric nature of Kung Fu was beginning to collapse and burst forth through China inundating the country with a multitude of styles and techniques. However, with such a surge of information much of the art aspect of Kung Fu was lost. For one thing, many of the secret styles and techniques remained secret; also due to the lack of written records, there was much individual interpretation; and finally, after leaving the monasteries, and becoming part of the people, the philosophical aspects of Zen (Ch'an) and meditation which made up such a necessary part of the art became extinct.

As the socio-political unrest continued, the temples became a haven for anti-dynastic activity and as a result they were subjected to numerous burnings. The monks fled to various parts of China and further disseminated their knowledge of Kung Fu.

1271-1368 A.D. . . . Yüan (Mongol Dynasty) . . . During this period, over 100,000 fighters rebelled against the Mongols in favor of a pure Sung government and now it seemed Kung Fu became a nucleus of popular resistance against the myriad of hostile dynasties, and a large percentage of the population became involved in the martial arts.

1368-1644 A.D. . . . the Ming Dynasty . . . . Shaolin fighting reached its peak during this period, but more important, underwent a revolutionary change that completed altered the Kung Fu style. Chang San-feng, a Taoist monk, observed that the Shaolin style was not in keeping with the natural laws of health, nourishing, and hygiene. The style required an excess expenditure of energy. He, therefore, instituted a modification of the old hard style, and so introduced the element of softness. It was so overwhelmingly accepted by the monks, that the harder Shaolin form almost vanished. It was not until 1522, that the hard style was revitalized by three great fighters.

It was through the efforts of three men, Kioh Yuan, Pai Yu Fong and an elderly man named Li, who pooled their knowledge and skills, that the hard style was not forever lost to history. They spent many years at the Shaolin monastery, attempting to reestablish the principles of the older Shaolin forms. They finally arrived at a system they called the Five Form Fist, based on the available information. It was fashioned after the dragon, tiger, leopard, snake and the stork.

About 1375, the threat of the Northern Manchurian tribes was eminent. The military leaders seeing the advantage of weaponless defense, organized the art and incorporated it into their military training. Up to this period, there was, of course, much information on other military techniques as the sword, staff, ax and archery. But now it was a complete system, with the introduction of empty hand fighting. One man in particular, General Chi, organized a manual in which he presented an extremely detailed and workable account of self defense, which included styles, forms, methods, and techniques.

1644-1912 A.D. the Ch'ing Dynasty (Manchu) ...
Similar to the Barbarian invasions by the Huns,
Goths, Visigoths, etc., China finally fell into the
hands of its Northern enemies, the Manchu-
rians. Once the Manchu occupied the land, however, they were incapable of effectively governing it. Under the weak rule of these invaders,
China was without military power to resist
foreign aggression. In 1894-95, Japan waged
war on China and through a peace treaty, China
lost Korea, Okinawa, and other satellite ter-
ritories. At the same time, Britian wrestled Hong
Kong from China. So harrassed was China by
foreign intervention, she tried to establish a
closed door policy to traders. This resulted in a
joint British-French-German-American-Russian-
Italian-Japanese military expedition that
captured Peking and exacted a large indemnity.
At this time, many of the Chinese patriots united
and attempted to intimidate all foreigners, thus
giving rise to the historical Boxer Rebellion.

During the early years of the Manchu occupation, the fighting art went underground because
the Chinese did not wish to share their knowledge with the invaders. Many of the masters
refused to yield to the new government and took
refuge, along with officials and supporters of the
overthrown Ming Dynasty, to plot the overthrow
of the Manchu and the restoration of the Ming.
In the monasteries, the art was practiced during
the early hours, so as not to be observed. To this
day, in many of the monasteries, this tradition
persists. Because of the many revolutionary activities, the temples were invaded, destroyed,
and burned to the ground. The boxers who

managed to escape, along with thousands of other fighters, retreated Southward and to Taiwan and so spread the gospel of the fighting arts to all corners of China. The Manchu, excellent warriors themselves, kept the Ming dissidents under control and imposed on all, the badge of subservience . . . the queue . . . which symbolized a horse's tail. The uprisings by the antidynastic Mings were so frequent and so violent that a governmental order . . . the Ching Edict of 1730 . . . was enacted to extinguish the flames of the martial arts.

As a result of the edict, Kung Fu appeared to fall out of the public eye and apparently vanished . . . . its remnants were visible only as calisthenic forms. In truth, however, the arts continued to thrive in clandestine quarters and were propagated from generation to generation. Finally during the Boxer Rebellion of 1900, the martial arts were totally eliminated from the Chinese mainland.

In the early 1900's a secret society of boxers united in an attempt to harrass and drive out of China, the foreigners who were preying on a weakened China. Initially, the Empress Dowager supported the boxers, however, when the fall of Peking was imminent, she turned against them and without imperial support, the Boxer Rebellion suffered a disastrous defeat. She attempted to forever destroy the strength and position of the boxers. She cleared all the training halls, executed all the leaders, and virtually eliminated the martial arts from the middle kingdom.

1912 A.D. . . . the Republic of China . . . . the yoke of the Manchu was finally thrown off, and a return to many of the traditional institutions of China was in vogue. At this time, boxing flowered and was initiated in all areas of Chinese learning.

1917-1927 . . . Warlord Period . . . China once again became a land of devastation and pillage, and was torn amongst an endless list of warlords, each proclaiming their right of leadership. The boxers of the kingdom were equally divided amongst these innumerable factions.

1928 . . . the War arts were renamed . . . Wu-Shu or war arts was now called Kuo Su or national arts and now boxing became formalized and nationalized.

Following World War II, and the Communists rise to power on the Mainland, many boxers retreated South to Taiwan with Chiang Kai-shek, to Hong Kong, and many other places, thus disseminating the seeds of the fighting arts throughout the world.

In concluding this section, I hope I have presented some of the political and social undercurrents which were influential in the evolution of Chinese Boxing, as well as cultivated a feeling or better understanding of Chinese culture.

Throughout its history, China has been a land torn with political havoc and endless wars. The many wars of the T'ang, Sung, Ming, Han, and Ch'ing dynasties were important in both promoting and destroying the martial arts. Because of these wars, the esoteric nature of the art was dissolved; more people were trained in shorter periods of time; and finally the art was disseminated to satellite continents and finally to the world.

Because of these and many other reasons, the art of Kung Fu has been made available to all people and the propagation of Chinese self defense, though still in its embryonic state, will sweep the world with a philosophy and culture that will have a profound effect on the lives of millions.

Socio-Political Highlights

c. 2873 B.C. Emperor Fu Shi .. nationalized medicine throughout China. Supposedly created the trigrams from which the hexagrams are derived, based on his observations of heaven, earth, animals, and man.

c. 2752 B.C. Emperor Shun Nung. . responsible for the classification of herbs, for medicinal use.

c. 2677 B.C. Emperor Huang Ti .. the legendary Yellow Emperor .. sent healers throughout China. First mention of "Go-ti" in the literature.

1111-249 B.C. . . The Chou Dynasty . . Book of Rites . . mentions the martial arts and healthier exercises as developed by Taoist monks. Spring and Autumn Annals and the Literature of the Warring States speak of archery, fencing, wrestling. King Wen codified the trigram symbols thus laying the foundation for the I-Ching.

206 B.C.-220 A.D. Han Dynasty

32-92 A.D. Pan Kuo . . wrote the Han Book of the Arts concerning logistics

c. 220 A.D. Dr. Hua To . . wrote the "Shou Pu" series of exercises based on animal movements.

618-907 A.D. Tang Dynasty . . "Go-ti" exported to Japan, modified, and becomes the basis of Jumo wrestling.

960-1297 . . Sung Dynasty . . China's age of Chivalry and the period of the heroics of the fighting monks

1271-1368 . . Yuan . . Mongol Dynasty . . . Shaloin temples and the fighting monks become a nucleus of resistance to the Mongols.

1368-1644 . . Ming Dynasty . . Shaolin fighting reached its zenith

1644-1912 . . Ch'ing Dynasty . . Manchu . . Invasion and take-over of the kingdom by the Manchu. Foreign intervention and exploitation adds to the weakness and instability of the country China's war with Japan 1894-1895 . . China loses Korea and Okinawa to Japan

1912 . . Republic of China . . overthrow of the Manchu . . boxing flourishes

1917-1927 . . Warlord period . . further political unrest and turmoil

1928 . . nationalization of the fighting arts

1949 . . People's republic

The Origin of Kung Fu

Before discussing the origin of Kung Fu, it becomes necessary to more clearly define the term. As mentioned earlier, in the old Chinese culture, Kung

Transmigration of the martial arts

Fu referred to the work and hours that were necessary for the accomplishment of a task; anyone who had dedicated much time and effort to gain proficiency was spoken of as being possessed of Kung Fu. Eventually, the term was used in reference to the fighting arts in general. As the term migrated to the West, it became generic for all fighting systems, rather than a specific style. Also in the west, the commercial world has had its influence on the interpretation of the word. With the growing popularity of many styles, the semantics of the art has become extremely ambiguous and the term Kung Fu has been applied as convenience dictates.

In any case, tracing the origin of the martial arts style associated with the term Kung Fu, Shaolin Fighting, Kempo etc., would fall into the same general classification. Bearing this in mind I will outline the origin and development of Kung Fu as it is recognized by the contemporary western culture.

Its origin is evolved over many many years of Chinese history, and represents a physical and psychological manifestation of a profound and ancient Chinese philosophy. It involves countless unsubstantiated facts, and countless unsubstantiated dates and figures, all of which were amalgamated to form an endless series of myths and legends which are called the origin of Kung Fu.

Historically, the chronology and authenticity of the art is extremely nebulous. It consists of an incomplete list of names, dates and events which have been altered by numerous vocal recountings. Its evolution is filled with ambiguities, contradictions, and lack of continuity as owing to its esoteric and in many cases clandestine development. Founded on a cornerstone of religion and philosophy, initiated as a health form by Taoist and Buddhist monks, intermingled with physical therapy and practices of hygiene and meditation, it evolved into the beautiful martial arts system, Kung Fu.

The development of Kung Fu is analagous to the formation of a mighty river at the base of a mountain. Trickling down the side of the mountain are numerous small streams, each no larger than the other, originating from non-specific areas throughout the peak. As they race towards the bottom of the mountain, their intensity and size increases as one joins another. Finally, at the base of the mountain, there is a convergence of all the streams. They flow together, forming one large, strong, smooth flowing river. As this river proceeds downward, it sends off many tributaries, each traveling its own independent journey, but yet, born of the mother source, thus sharing with each other a common unity.

The innumerable stories and legends surrounding the beginnings of Kung Fu are endless. I have listed the better known of these legends knowing not which is fact and which is fiction. It is in the hands of the reader to develop any attitude he wishes, bearing in mind that all legend is founded to some degree on fact, and in presenting a historical synopsis such as this, it is almost impossible to separate one from the other.

Most historians credit the origin of Kung Fu to a Buddhist Monk, Bodidharuma, who developed the forerunner of the style in the Shaolin monastery.

The first Shaolin temple was built by Emperor Wsiao Wen (386-534). It is believed to have been constructed on the northern side of Shao-shih mountain, in Honan Province, south of Sung Mountain. Legend describes it as a magnificent edifice containing twelve upper and lower courts. It lay in a beautiful setting, high on the mountain surrounded with trees of every variety, interspersed with the quiet rippling of brooks and picturesque waterfalls. Here it is said, Bodhiruchi translated Buddhist scripture into Chinese ... and here also is where Tamo (Bodhidarma) meditated, introduced his Zen teachings and helped cultivate Chinese boxers.

There are two theories concerning Tamo and his effect on the Shaolin system. The first holds that he introduced the fighting system to the temple monks,

Kung Fu—a "river" of martial arts uniting many "streams."

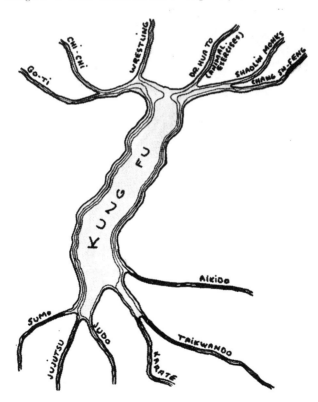

and the second school contends that the Shaolin monks were widely reknowned for their fighting ability, as shown by their astonishing skill on the battlefields of previous eras, and that Tamo influenced their style with his sinew changing and marrow washing instruction.

In any case, according to legend, their lived in India, in the sixth century (C. 520) a Buddhist monk named Bodhidharma, also known as Tamo. He was the son of King Sugandha and was an excellent warrior who had received his martial arts training from an old master, Prajnatara. Tamo was extremely strong, very disciplined and in excellent physical condition as owing to a series of exercises he had developed.

Tamo left India, crossed the Himalayan mountains and traveled to China to spread his teachings of Zen. During the reign of Emperor Leungwuti (c. 520 A.D.) he arrived in Northern China in the province of Honan where he entered the Shaolin Monastery of Mt. Shung. Reportedly, he sat for nine years facing a wall, and "listened to the ants scream." He was looked upon as a man of almost demonic spiritual power. Once while meditating, he fell asleep, and became so enraged, he ripped off his eyelids, and threw them to the ground. Immediately there arose tea shrubs, whose leaves were used by the monks to keep them awake.

The monks were very interested in his teachings. However due to their poor physical condition, were unable to stay awake during his classes. He therefore sought to improve their degenerate bodies by instituting a practice of health nourishing exercises. The three courses he taught were called "the Eighteen Movements of the Ahran Hands," "Sinew Changing Exercises" and "Marrow Washing Exercises." These were designed to improve their health, and assist their meditation. The emphasis was on rhythmic breathing, coupled with bending and stretching of the body. Ultimately, these exercises became the forerunner of Shaolin boxing. Although their purpose as an exercise was fully realized, there was an obvious side benefit . . . . that of self defense. Since the monks at Shaolin were in constant physical danger, and were by their religious code forbidden to bear weapons, they modified many of the exercises to form a highly sophisticated system of weaponless defense. This Shaolin boxing method initially involved the hard, stiff, fast kicking, fast punching forms of self defense and came to be known as the hard school of Chinese boxing.

Up to this time, Chinese boxing was a loosely organized series of unrelated forms. However, due to the efforts of Tamo, the art adopted a degree of unification. Reportedly he left two manuscripts, only one of which has come down to us. . . . "the Muscle Change Classic or the I-Chin Ching."

These exercises and forms eventually found their way out of the monasteries. Many of the merchants passing through the mountains would learn these exercises in order to better protect themselves from attacks by road bandits and thieves. They passed these secrets on to other merchants who in turn passed it on to their families. Each transition involved refinements and modifications and thus arose the various schools of the art.

Up to the time of the Manchurian invasion, the Shaolin temple was a habitat for the religious, however, with the end of the Ming Dynasty, the temple became a refuge for the Ming officials and revolutionaries. These men shaved their heads, adorned the clothing of a priest, and so assumed the role of a monk to evade the Manchu. Their names were virtually scratched from the family scrolls and they were no longer subjected to the laws of family or state, and became "servants of god." The Manchu, who were nomads like the Mongols of the previous dynast, were very superstitious and so avoided all religious involvement. As a result, these Ming officials were left pretty much alone. Hence, there were two types of priests in the Shaolin temple . . . the true monks who were looking for salvation of the soul, and the loyalists who trained fighters for the restoration of the Ming Dynasty. Eventually, however, they were found out. The temple was surrounded . . . . the monks fought valiantly against overwhelming odds. Most of them were killed. The few that escaped fled to South China where they founded a second Shaolin monastary in the province of Fukien to recruit and train members for the same revolutionary purpose.

Perfection of the art in the monastery was mandatory. The students underwent several rigid tests to graduate. Many times they failed, in which case they stayed on until they were able to successfully meet the requirements. The test was three-fold. The first part was an oral examination involving the history and principles underlying the art. The second part involved actual physical competition in which one student was pitted against one or more students. The third and final part was the most rigorous and gruelling. It was a hazardous life or death test.

The student was led to a specially designed labyrinth in which were prepared 108 series of systematically mechanized dummies, snares, and traps. The dummies were equipped with clenched wooden fists, staffs, knives, spears and other lethal devices. Each of these traps would react in an unpredictable manner, and were triggered by the boards on which the student walked. Often he would step on more than one board and so trigger more than one dummy. His life depended on his ability and split second response. Finally, when and if he reached the end of the labyrinth, which was at the temple front gate, he was confronted with one final test. Blocking the doorway was a huge smoldering urn, filled with flaming coals. To gain his freedom, he was required to move the urn by hugging it with his forearms, thus branding himself with two symbols . . . one of a dragon and one of a tiger . . . . the highly respected and revered marks of a Shaolin monk.

Thus far, we have seen the evolution of the hard school of Shaolin temple boxing. To be sure, there is some basis of fact in the presentation, however, interspersed throughout, are many references to legend, but as previously mentioned, most legend is based to some degree on fact.

Shaolin fighting was not the ultimate development in self-defense. For not long afterwards, coinciding with a greater appreciation of the deep philosophical principles underlying Shaolin boxing, a new form evolved. It was found that instead of being necessary to use great muscular effort, that by calming the mind and putting the body into a completely relaxed state of equilibrium, one could more fully yield to the opponent, thus realizing more completely the principles of yin and yang. The movements of the hard Shaolin boxing were adapted to this new thinking and thus arose the perfect blend of the hard and soft styles thus instituting the complete self defense style, Kung Fu.

The introduction of the soft style into the arts was a revelation of one Chang San-feng. But before elucidating on this monk, let me first define what is meant by the soft style.

Of the soft style there are three main branches . . . Pa-kua, which consists mainly of circular evasion and mostly open palm attack; Hsing-i, which stresses vertical or linear movement and direct hair trigger attack on a straight line, like a rolling wave and Tai Chi, which is characterized by subtle yeilding with circular evasion and attack. The soft school techniques can best be compared to the ancient sport of Chinese kite fighting. In this ancient Chinese sport, the opponents fought with kites which flew high in the air. The strings holding the kites were specially prepared. They were resined and sugared with crushed glass. In this manner, the string of one could easily sever the string of an opponent. In a match, which in many cases lasted for hours, the key to victory was to keep one's line slack so that the opponent was unable to sever it. Conversely, when the opponent's line became taut, it was a simple matter to cut the string, sending his kite off into the sky, thus winning the match. One can easily see the analogy with boxing . . . once a man looses his softness, he became an easy mark for his opponent. The method is simple enough . . be relaxed . . . but most difficult to carry out in the heat of combat. But the ancients thought it well worth the effort, if for nothing more than the discipline it imposed.

From the above, we can easily see the tone of the soft or internal school. "Internal, as the word implies is the control of one's self through internal discipline . . . it involves the ability to slow down . . . to quiet the nervous system by a direct act of the will . . . there is a conscious lowering of one's ch'i or intrinsic energy. In this tranquil state, all distracting thoughts are shut out . . . the mind and the body are sharpened but at ease in a peaceful quiet state."

Up to this period in time, fighting was a purely

hard style. But now we have the element of softness being introduced and these two facets, hardness and softness, were united to form the complete system of fighting, Kung Fu.

As an outgrowth of this development, there is a school of thought that credits Chang San-feng as the father of Kung Fu. It concedes that Tamo and his Buddhist monks laid the foundation for the style, however, feel that it did not reach maturity until Chang added the necessary component of softness.

In the 13th century, a Taoist monk, Chang San-feng, known as the immortal, left his capacity as a government official to become a hermit. He studied under various Taoists, traveling from place to place, learning the techniques of meditation and the martial arts. It was while spending a night in a monastery, that he realized that utilizing great muscular strength and energy was not in keeping with the laws of nature and hygiene. He felt that by calming the mind, and controlling the ch'i so as to put the mind and body into a completely relaxed state of equilibrium, one could more completely utilize the principles of yin and yang, and so realize a greater effectiveness with the expenditure of less energy.

One night, Chang had a dream in which God showed him how to fight: in this dream he killed hundreds of people. He pondered many days on his dream as he walked through the courtyards meditating. One afternoon, as he was reading in his room, he was distracted by an unfamiliar disturbance in the lower courtyard. He ran to his window and saw a snake engaged in combat with a crane. As the snake hissed a challenge to his opponent, the crane swooped down from the tree, his wings in full spread, and struck at the snake with his sharp pointed beak. The snake responded by curling his head in and lashing at the crane with his tail. The crane parried the strike by lifting his leg and thwarted the snake's tail with his wing. Then the crane attacked with both claws. Again the snake was able to avoid this attack by twisting and curling. Finally, after tiring themselves out, the two combatants called a draw as the crane flew back to its perch in the tree and the snake slithered away.

Chang watched this performance from his window again and again. Finally he realized the value of yielding the force of strength .... also he realized the value of a continuity of movement. In the combat of the crane and the snake, he saw in living form the principle of the I-Ching .... the strong changing to the yielding and the yielding changing to the strong. He remembered Lao Tzu's analogy of the yielding water and the hard stone. The great master studied the crane and the snake, wild animals, clouds, water, and trees bending in the wind. He codified these natural movements and made them a part of an exercise system. From the action of the crane arose "White Crane Spreads Wings." From the action of the snake arose "Snake Creeps Down." The crane attacking with its beak give us "Brush Knee and Twist." Constructing other forms based on the movements he had seen, he also adapted Shaolin martial arts to the Taoist meditation.

Chang taught his disciples Taoism and meditation in the White Clouded Temple in the Peking West Mountains. He created a school for his system on the Wu Tang Mountains. This was known as the Wu Tang School which developed his system of self-defense.

In the 16th century, a wealthy young boxer, Kwok Yuen, entered the Shaolin temple to increase his knowledge of the fighting arts. He spent many years

The crane and snake in combat employ the principles of I-Ching . . . each in turn yielding in the force of strength.

there, absorbing all the information he could and developed many techniques. He studied particularly Tamo's original 18 exercises and after much experimentation he expanded these forms into seventy-two exercises. Realizing his limitations and lack of experience, he recognized the incompleteness of the system. He ventured across China in search of more knowledge with which he could perfect the style. In a small town in Southern China, he met an excellent fighter, Pak Yook Fong, and an old master called Li. He spoke with them and learned they had developed an open hand claw technique. Eager to learn as much as he could, he challenged Pak to a friendly contest and was so impressed with his style, that he invited both the men to return to the temple with him. There the three men expanded the 72 movements into 170 and then they divided these into five distinct styles . . . . the Tiger, Crane, Snake, Leopard and Dragon. These styles formed the basis of the Five Form Fist which many historians credit as the Kung Fu Style.

In the eighteenth century, a boxer, Hung Hee Gung became a disciple of two famous Shaolin monks. One a master of the long hand boxing, Chee Sin and the other a master of the short hand style, Fong Wing Chuen. Hung became extremely proficient in both styles and eventually combined the best methods of both, to form a fighting style of his own. After having perfected this system, he taught it to his disciples who passed it on from generation to generation being sure the techniques of the Five Form Fist were retained. Today his school Hung Kuen, Hu Hok Pai is referred to as the original school of Shaolin Kung Fu.

These are just a few of the numerous stories which are involved in the origin of Kung Fu. Some are fact, some are legend, some part fact and part legend. Because of a lack of records, because of the esoteric nature of the art, because of the numerous vocal re-countings, who is to say which of these stories is credulous, and which is not. In any case, we can be certain of the following data as being an accurate account of the origin and evolution of Kung Fu.

Fighting as a complete art originated during the period of the Legendary Yellow Emperor c. 2600 B.C. with the development of an interest in hygiene and longevity. During this same period, we have a record of the first contest in history, the "go-ti" dance which evolved into a form of wrestling. The "go-ti" dance ultimately evolved into a form of primitive wrestling. It later was utilized in both boxing and wrestling. As the medical aspect was further developed, a more accurate knowledge of anatomy and physiology was realized and this knowledge found its way into the monasteries and was coupled with the previously existing exercises of health, hygiene and fighting. In the 5th century, B.C., the advent of Taoism, Confucianism, and Buddhism added much impact to the evolution of the fighting arts in the monastaries and contributed the spiritual elements of breathing and meditation. However it was not until the arrival of Bodidharuma (c. 520 A.D.), that the art reached a degree of unification. The previously hard Shaolin style was devoid of any spiritual influence, and now was indoctrinated with the philosophical and religious aspects of Zen which made it not only an excellent fighting style but also a religious rite whereby the mind and body were in perfect harmony.

Now the Shaolin Temple became a hub of activity for the martial arts. Originally this knowledge was confined to the walls of the monastery, and restricted to the religious monks, because not only was it considered part of a religious rite, but also it was recognized as a deadly art and the monks were not eager to arm the people of China with such a weapon.

Eventually the esoteric nature of the art started to dwindle, and the trickling knowledge found its way first to the merchants passing through and second as a result of many wars during the Tang, Sung, Ming, and Ching dynasties. Out of necessity the people were trained initially to defend themselves against the bandits and thieves, and finally against the innumerable hostile dynasties.

During the Ming Dynasty (1368-1644), the martial arts reached an excellence of development. The one missing component was the contribution of a Taoist Monk. Up to this time, expertise in Kung Fu was dependent upon speed and strength, which was not in keeping with the principles of health and Taoism, and not in accord with the nature of things. And so Chang San-feng (1279-1368), observed the importance of the principles of softness and of yielding, and of continuity of movement thereby embodying the philosophical principles of Yin and Yang. These concepts were made an intregal part of the previously hard Shaolin Kung Fu and now for the first time, we have the perfect art founded on a perfect union of mind, body, and spirit.

After this period, growth of Kung Fu was either increased or diminished, depending on the whims of the dynasties. As a military pawn, it lost much of the spiritual element which was such a necessary and integral part of the art. Also because of expediency the men who were trained were taught quickly and without the necessary knowledge to make the art effective, and so again much of the art was lost. Many of the occupational dynasties recognized the political influence the boxers wielded, and often tried to snuff the flame of the martial arts. However they had become such an integral and vital part of the Chinese Culture that in the end its tenacity overcame all pressure attempting to eliminate Kung Fu.

As the years passed, much of the original style was lost . . . what was left became modified and/or misinterpreted by many of its disciples. Proficiency in one aspect led to the creation of specialties, and finally arose a multitude of forms and styles each claiming to be the original Kung Fu. What is taught as Kung Fu today, I'm sure, may have remnants of the original form, but the difference between what is authentic and what is stylized will never be known.

The HARD and
the SOFT SCHOOLS

In the Chinese martial arts system there are two recognized styles. . . . the hard or external school and its offshoot, the Nei Chia or soft, internal school. The hard school has become synonomous with Shaolin Temple Boxing. Both these schools have been influential in the development of Kung Fu and I feel a cursory examination of the two, will be most beneficial in developing our theme.

Kung Fu is a perfect blend of both the hard and the soft styles. I would like to discuss these two aspects and present their merits and their differences. I'm sure this will give the reader a better understanding and appreciation of the beauty of Kung Fu.

The most significant differences between the hard and the soft school are two-fold. . . . they are the physical differences and the metaphysical differences.

As we know from our previous readings, the hard school consisted of the hard kicking, striking and punching techniques in which strength and speed determine the proficiency of the fighter. In the soft school, though the efficacy of the strike is far superior and results in a greater penetration, the movements appear to be smooth and continuous. Of the three main branches of the soft school. . . . Pa-Kua, Hsing-i, and Tai Chi . . . the latter best exemplifies the internal or soft school.

One of the many legends surrounding the system of Tai Chi speaks of Yang Pan-hou (1838-1881), son of Yang Lu-ch'an, one of the original founders of Tai Chi Chuan. Yang was involved in a quarrel concern-

ing the merits of the soft style and so was challenged
to a contest. The contest was held in the village square
and drew thousands of spectators as both the men involved were extremely proficient. Liu, a highly skilled
hard style fighter and Yang, equally proficient in the
soft style techniques. The contest, ultimately, was to
determine which of the two styles was superior, and
so drew the interest of thousands from miles around.

Finally, as the sun reached its zenith, the spectators
quieted down and the two contestants approached
the center of the village. The battle continued late
into the afternoon, as both men were equally proficient in parrying the attack of the other. Finally, Liu,
was able to land a stunning blow at Yang's neck. Instinctively, Yang responded, rolled back and at the
same time grasped Liu's wrist and threw him to the
ground. Liu lay there for a few seconds, gasping for
air and then fell into unconsciousness. Yang had won.
The crowd rose to its feet shouting and cheering
both fighters. Then they raised Yang to their shoul-
ders and formed a victory procession marching
through town singing songs of praise. The march
ended at Yang's house. Yang, extremely happy with
his victory, related a description of the contest to
his father. The elder Yang smiled. Then he lifted his
eyes to his son and said, "You have done well, my
son, but your sleeve is torn. . . . is this in keeping with
our principles of softness."

What the old man meant, of course, is that the soft
art is not in keeping with the hard movement indigenous to the hard style, but rather is a fluid, tranquil
art dependent upon a settling of the mind in harmony with the body thus resulting in the smooth continuous motion of Tai Chi.

Remembering that the soft style is predicated on
the overall health and longevity of the fighter, it is not

difficult to see that the hard will burn itself out in a relatively short time as we can see so easily in the productive lifespan of many of our contemporary athletes. On the other hand, a practitioner of the soft style will be able to perform effectively even into the late stages of his life.

The physical differences between the hard and the soft school are many. Listed are just a few in order to show more clearly this distinction. In the hard school, strength is derived from muscularity and hardness; whereas in the soft school, strength is derived from a balance of the internal organs and a control of the ch'i. The soft school spurns both bravery and force. Correct application hinges entirely on the mind. "To take advantage of impending motion and momentum so as to deflect the impetus of a thousand pounds with a trigger force of four ounces." In addition to relaxing completely and avoiding the uses of muscular force, the student of the internal school must "give himself up and yield before his opponent." This sounds incredible to the orthodox boxer. To surrender one's body to full relaxation and to yield to the opponent. . . . is this not courting disaster? But if the student fails to heed this advice, he is certain to fail. To illustrate, when a Tai Chi expert meets an opponent, he neither resists nor counters the blow, instead, he yields before the force, thus taking advantage of his opponent's momentum, and adds a push or pull so that with the augmented impetus, the opponent meeting no resistance is thrown to the ground. This is how a mere four ounces can topple a thousand pounds. The four ounces do not defeat the thousands pounds, of course, but rather causes the heavier force to defeat itself. This action exemplifies the concept of "giving up oneself and yielding before the opponent." To summarize:

hard or external	soft or internal
stresses physical and external muscle size and achievement and pragmatic postures, flamboyant display and demonstration of strength.	combined training or spirit and body as exemplified in the doctrines of Buddhism and Taoism. Spiritual culturation is very important, setting aside worldly desires and arrogant aggressive attitude.
hard and vigorous	soft and pliable
relies on muscular force and physical bravery and speed	spurns both bravery and force and relies on sensitivity
utilizes the force of the limbs	body is one piece, hence the resultant force is greater
answers force with force	turns opponents force against him and uses it to defeat him
no refinement	very refine, hence more in keeping with the philosophy of art
concerned with development of bulky muscles, enlargement of the chest, show of masculinity and relies on strength, force and vigorous movements	relies on the health of the internal organs, balance and poise, external attitude and gentility

| hence, is suited to the | hence is suited to all |
| young. | ages. |

If the physical development of the soft style represents the right arm of the martial arts, then certainly, the metaphysical and/or philosophical contributions represent the left arm. The soft style of the martial arts is unique in that unlike any other martial arts system, it is based on the physical, but also on the psychological manifestation of the profound ancient Chinese philosophy. These teachings embody the Tao, the I-Ching, Zen and Confucianism. Therefore, we can see the total and magnificent impact that the soft style had on the development of Kung Fu as the complete martial arts system. . . . a union of the moral, spiritual and physical.

Metaphysically, the hard schools had no basis in philosophy, but were concerned only with the aggressive aspects. On the other hand, the soft schools evolved over many years of profound and ancient Chinese philosophy encompassing the I-Ching, Taoism, Buddhism. Thus it stands above all other martial arts which have to philosophical support and has become the perfect art, blending all three aspects of man. . . . the moral, the spiritual, and the physical.

For the purpose of chronological orientation, we will use Lao Tzu (c. 611 B.C.) as our reference point. For during his life span there was a union of the Chinese mind which up to now had been clamoring for a unification of religion and philosophy that was directly related to the socio-political unrest of the time.

In 771 B.C. the Chou dynasty was forced out of its capitol by the Northern barbarians and so began a long period of anarchy, wars, pillage, tyranny, and slaughter which lasted over 500 years. Feudal monarchs lost control over their vassals . . . neighbor warred with neighbor, city state fought with city state, and finally about 479 B.C., the Chou dynasty lay prostrate under the ravages of turmoil. From the 5th century B.C. on, there ensued a ruthless struggle for power which ended in 221 B.C. at which time the Ch'in became the great military power of China after a series of campaigns. So bloody were these wars, that in one single campaign, 400,000 prisoners were decapitated. Finally in 221 B.C. the duke of ch'in became the first emperor of China, an event he celebrated in 213 by burning all the books in the empire except those on longevity, medicine, and agriculture. Now war ceased to be a noble exercise. Slaughter and tyranny reigned; alliances were formed and dissolved, wars were followed by more wars, and armies marched to and fro over the lands, ravaging and pillaging. This was the period of the fighting states.

These were the times in which Lao Tzu lived, and being bothered by the inevitable rape of his country, he tried to help the people and save China through a reorientation of the philosophical outlook.

According to legend, Lao Tzu was born c. 600 B.C. He instituted a completely different concept to his people arising out of a need of the times, and so became the founding father of Taoism. Only those principles of interest in developing the metaphysical theme of the soft style are mentioned here. Lao Tzu's answer to the existing strife and anarchy was as follows:

   a) He introduced the doctrine of Wu Wei . . . or inaction. He felt the best method of coping with the problem was to do nothing. Believing that force defeats itself, he held that if we interfere with a creature's existence, it will actively resist as a stone resists crushing. But a living creature grows stronger as the interference grows. Stronger . . . therefore . . . if a ruler tries to impose his will on the people, the result will be just opposite his objectives. An extension of this is the theory that . . . "the soft overcomes the hard and the weak overcomes the strong." Lao Tzu uses his favorite metaphor . . . water, "which of all things is most yielding. . . . but can overwhelm the rock which of all things is most hard." Richard Nixon, upon hearing his brother quarrelling with his father said to him, "just don't argue with him and you'll have a better chance of getting what you want."

Lao's doctrine does not imply that all action is to be avoided, but rather all hostile aggressive action.

  b) Lao's second underlying doctrine is that of the "Uncarved Block" . . . P'u. Man must return to his original nature . . . like that of the newborn child . . . naturally simple and good, free from hostility and aggression. Society as it exists has marred man's original nature, thus disfiguring it and making of man a competitive, aggressive, fierce animal. To return to this original nature required two disciplines:

    1. Cultivate an ideology of "fewness of desires". . . i.e., desire of money, power, self esteem, etc.

    2. Rejection of public opinion . . . which is a powerful motivating force which influences many of the competitive instincts of man. To reach the uncarved block is to "know oneself."

It should be recognized that these two precepts of Lao are also employed as the basic undercurrent of the soft style of Chinese boxing, and so clearly relates the art form to the Chinese philosophy which so greatly altered Chinese thinking.

In lauding the important characteristics of the internal system, Lao Tzu in his Tao Te Ching says of his philosophy:

> "Nothing under heaven is softer or more yielding than water; but when it attacks things hard and resistant, there is no way of altering it. That the yielding conquers the resistant and the soft overcomes the hard is a fact known by all men . . . yet utilized by none."

Further he says:

> "Can you, when concentrating your breath, make it soft, like that of a child . . . that is called the Mysterious Power."

Further:

> "A man is supple and weak when living, but hard and stiff when dead. Grass and trees are pliant and fragile when living, but dried and shriveled when dead. Thus the hard and the strong are the comrades of death; the supple and weak are the conrades of life."

> "Great squareness has no corners;
> great talents ripen late;
> great music is soft
> great form is shapeless."

> "To yield is to be preserved whole;
> to be bent is to become straight;
> to be hollow is to be filled;
> to be tattered is to be renewed;
> to have little is to gain;
> to have much is to be confused."

> "Without contention comes easy victory;
> without call comes what is deserved."

"A good soldier is not violent;
a good fighter does not rage;
a good conquerer does not give battle;
a good commander is a humble man."

"He who knows others is clever;
he who knows himself has insight;
he who conquers others has force;
he who conquers himself is truly strong."

"The softest substance in the world,
     goes through the hardest;
that which is without form
     penetrates that which has no crevice."
"The weak overcomes the strong;
the soft overcomes the hard;
this is known by all
but practiced by none."

And Finally:
"When the best student hears about the way,
     he practices it assiduously;
When the average student hears about the way,
     it seems to him, one moment there, and
gone the
          next;
When the worst student hears about the way,
     he laughs out loud;
If he did not laugh,
     It would be unworthy of being the way."
From these few passages of Lao Tzu's Tao Te
Ching, one can readily see the relationship of his
teachings to the Chinese mind but also the tremen-
dous impact and influence his words exerted on
Chinese martial arts. The previously hard, unyield-
ing, aggressive Shaolin style was about to absorb the
principles of softness, yielding and continuity of

movement that would make it a complete style or rather the style of Kung Fu.

Of course there were other metaphysical influences that were absorbed into the philosophy of fighting. For example, Lao's successor Chuang Tzu, also spoke of the merits of softness in movement, emphasizing such properties as the will (i) and the vital energy (chi).

Mencius, a contemporary of Chuang Tzu also believed in the force of the will and its complement the ch'i . . . but believed they could be cultivated only through right and proper living.

Complimenting the action of "i" and "ch'i" were the Taoist doctrined of "wu wei" and "tzu-jan." Wu wei means to refrain from contention and tzu-jan implied a natural response, instinctive to the attacking force. Hence, the foundations of the internal system were established. . . . the will, vital energy, effortlessness, and spontaneity.

The growing body of hygiene doctrine that was gaining much momentum in China, was augmented by the philosophy of Buddhist monks arriving in China from India. One of the most profound and influential developments of these monks was the doctrine of Zen or Ch'an as taught by Tamo (c. 500 A.D.).

After this period in history, the socio-religious reforms introduced by Lao, permeated throughout China with such explosive speed, that by 184 A.D. most of the country had been converted. The new religious philosophy gave rise to a multitude of branches such as alchemy, and hygiene as related to the universe and to Taoism. . . . and as many disciples of these adjunctive philosophies. Concurrent with these offshoots of Taoism, preoccupation with health and longevity became almost obsessive with the Chinese and was a very strong influence in their lives.

Again, let us not loose sight of the relationship of these doctrines with the martial arts, as they were all influential in the development of the new style. One of the most influential physicals extolling the merits of this philosophy of health, hygiene and longevity during this period, was Dr. Hua To (c. 220 A.D.) who introduced his exercises fashioned after the movements of animals.

Between 350 B.C. and 250 B.C., during the ages of Lao Tzu and his followers Chuang Tzu and Lieh Tzu, there came into being hundreds of hygiene schools. These schools cultivated longevity through breathing and gymnastics. Chuang Tzu himself, atttibuted many of his powers to his idealized way of life and his purity of breath. . . . ch'i.

Concurrent with these activities, new theories concerning health and hygiene and their relationship to religion were proposed. As far back as 100 B.C., the pursuit of immortality was strongly entrenched in Chinese culture and the firm conviction that body and breath must be kept in motion to prevent decay. Breathing became a religion in itself and its importance gave rise to a whole new school of thought that has permeated societies throughout the world. Hygiene itself, for many became a life's work and was so intricate and rigorous that it hardly permitted the adept to hold an ordinary job. Though physical immortality was not the objective of the Taoist, health was, and they believed immortality is no more than an extension of health. . . i.e., not physical immortality, but mere longevity.

Today in China, hygiene is still practiced. There is many an educated person who regularly lies down and concentrates on a point 1.3 inches below his naval. . . . quiets his respiration and meditates. These practices are thought to increase a man's resistance to disease and retard old age. They are not regarded as necessarily Taoist, however there is not doubt as to their origin.

During the 4th Century B.C. Lao Tzu's philosophy swept the country along with other deep Chinese philosophies. The principle of Yin and Yang, as well as the five elements (wu-hsing) and the interrelationship of these principles to man, spirit, health, hygiene, metaphysics and cosmology all played an equally important part in molding the philosophical and religious attitudes of the people.

The concepts of Yin and Yang and the five elements go far back into antiquity and of quite independent origins. Much obscurity still surrounds their history. We know these concepts existed long before 1200 B.C., and as early as 690 B.C. these theories were incorporated into the healing arts.

All of these ideologies ... yin and yang (which formed the basis of the 64 hexagrams), the 64 hexagrams themselves ... are all related to the I-Ching. ... the book of changes which forms another portion of our philosophical foundation.

The composition of the I-Ching is attributed to King Wen, the father and founder of the Chou Dynasty (1150-249 B.C.). He completed it at a time when the last Shang ruler held him captive.

The concept of change which gave the I-Ching its name and determines its system of thought is centered around two principles ... movement ... and the unchanging laws governing that movement. This movement or change is never one dimensional in direction. Cyclic movement is the best term, a movement that returns to its starting point, never stopping but continual and so passes into another movement.

The I-Ching is based on 64 hexagrams, each of which is composed of divided and undivided lines representative of nourishment, evolution, personality, social life, character traits, etc. Its purpose is analagous to the oracle, and so allows the reader to subjectively interpolate the answers to his questions and problems.

The creation of the trigrams which form the hexagrams is attributed to Fu Shi . . . the legendary Chinese Emperor and sage, who lived almost 5000 years ago. They are based on his observations of heaven, earth, animals and man. The creation of the 64 hexagrams is unclear, however, and legend maintains they were created sometime after Fu Chi.

In the 12th century B.C. King Wen codified these symbols during his captivity. He spent seven years in prison studying the hexagrams night and day. He structured his findings in the form of predictions.

His son, the Duke of Chou, completed the work. The last contribution to the I-Ching was made by the great Chinese philosopher, Confucius, who wrote a complete and detailed treatise on the philosophy of the book which he called the Ten Wings of the I-Ching.

The I-Ching has exerted an influence in China for over 3000 years. The individual hexagrams predate the book. They were preserved on wooden tablets long before they were recorded by King Wen.

Of such importance is this classic that it was the only one of the Five Confucian Classics to be spared when the Emperor Ch'in ordered all ancient books burned in 213 B.C. It has been a reference for both Confucian and Taoist philosophers for many centuries.

In the 11th century A.D., Chou Tung I (1016-1073) designed his diagram expressing the Yin Yang relationship, which has been adopted as the symbol of Kung Fu. He designed this diagram to represent the transmutation between these two opposite attributes Yin and Yang, and incorporated into its meaning the I-Ching or change, the five elements (wu-hsing), fire, water, metal, wood, and earth . . . and the eight diagrams.

The art of Kung Fu utilizes all the movements of the Ying-Yang circle, exhibiting that all the movements travel in circles which have no beginning or end, but also changeability, thus providing grace and dexterity to the art.

In closing this section of the martial arts, I would like to leave the reader with the following thoughts. Kung Fu is not a programmed robot-like self defense, but rather a style that is natural; natural to the order of things, natural to the principles of life, and natural to man himself. It is a conglomerate of ever changing factors. It is neither hard or soft. . . . but a perfect blend of the two. It is neither strictly health orientated or self-defense orientated . . . but again, a perfect blend of the two. It is neither a defense art nor an aggressive art but a perfect harmony of both these aspects. But more important than these physical concepts of Kung Fu are the metaphysical considerations.

In this chapter we have touched on religion, philosophy, cosmology, and theosophy. We have examined to some degree the ancient Chinese concepts of genesis and the attempts towards prognostication based on the systematized formula in which everything existing is broken down into an equation . . . the I-Ching. We have examined the philosophy of the great sages of Lao Tzu, and Fu Shi. We have seen the alterations of the fighting style from the extreme hard to the soft. We have, in fact, not only tried to show the differences between the hard and soft style, but also to show the effect that these styles, as well as a multitude of other influencing factors, have had on the evolution of Kung Fu.

Finally, basing our discourse on the thinking of the ancients, and particularly the I-Ching, we must bear in mind that nothing is in a state of static existence. Life is made up of a series of unending change which continues to infinity. The same line of thinking must be applied to Kung Fu. I'm sure at its conception it was believed to be the perfect martial art form. Likewise with the endless innovations, the art was subjected to, many times over, it was thought to be at its solstice. And so too even today, there is little doubt that some expert will undoubtedly add or detract some move or movements that in his eyes will make Kung Fu a superior style. But that is the way of man. . . . that is the way of life. . . . that is the way of the I-Ching.

Transmigration of the Martial Arts

Once the secrets of the martial arts had filtered out of the conclave of the monastary, the world was to receive the greatest gift of Chinese Culture ever. As Kung Fu traveled to distant lands, it was, however, subjected to various transmutations and alterations coinciding with the culture, ideology, philosophy, and topography of the new lands in which it took root. In many cases the name, Kung Fu was lost and gave way to translations into the local terminology. Also, it was often given an entirely new name, thus giving the fighting art a national flavor. Today, many of these fighting systems from other countries, even though all are indigenous to Kung Fu, show very little relationship to the Chinese system or Chinese terminology.

Based on (the) available bits and pieces of information scattered throughout the history of these countries, let us explore further how Chinese Kung Fu traveled to far off lands and in some cases evolved into what became the national sport of these lands.

Given a little license, it is not difficult to imagine one source of exportation of the art. Merchants passing through the monastary learned much of the self defense aspect of Kung Fu to protect themselves from the roadside bandits and thieves. As these merchants often crossed the borders of distant lands, this information of course, went with them. Philosophers, teachers, and monks spreading their doctrines, to the many distant towns and villages carried with them the seeds of the martial arts. Also, the military men scattered throughout the world were a source of carrying information from and to their native lands.

Historically, the earliest known exportation of Chinese self defense, was during the Tang Dynasty (618-907 A.D.). The "Go-ti" dance mentioned in an earlier chapter found its way to Japan and with some modification became the national sport of Japan, Sumo wrestling.

During the Japanese war with China, 1894-1895, China lost Korea and Okinawa to Japan and the Japanese being very quick to recognize the advantages of these systems absorbed all the information they could from these occupied Chinese islands.

Up to the period of the thirteen century A.D., the Japanese martial arts system evolved as part of the military combative aspects. It was a fighting style that was a conglomerate of many styles from many countries such as Sumo wrestling and Atemi. Atemi consisted of striking the vital points of the body and was a derivative of the Chinese Okinawan system, which was a direct descendant of Chinese Chuan-fa or empty hand. These are just two of the many foreign elements, which were coupled with the local military styles, that formed the Japanese combative system of empty hand fighting.

At this same time in China, under the Ming Dynasty (1368-1648), the development of the fighting arts had reached a high degree of sophistication. However when the Manchu invaded and occupied the country, not only did the art go underground, but also many of the great fighters fled to other countries, taking with them their knowledge of Chinese self defense and so scattered their many techniques to many of their Southeastern neighbors.

One Ming patriot, Chan Yuan-bin (also spelled Chen Yuan-ping), a particularly talented and knowledgeable monk, took refuge in the Bushiu Temple in Tokyo to teach Zen (ch'an) and meditation. Eventually, as part of the mental-physical aspect, he taught the Kung Fu arts. One of his pupils, Miura Yoshitatsu, became extremely adept at the Chinese style and gained recognition as Chan's best pupil. With his pre-existing knowledge of the martial arts, he was able to blend the best of Chinese Kung Fu, with the existing Japanese system. He incorporated many of the principles of softness and yielding. . . . particularly the excellent blocking methods and the way of the fast hand indigenous to the Shaolin Boxing methods. He took the best of both, combined the two and developed his own system which he called "jujutsu." To this day he is recognized as the founder of "Jujutsu."

Ju is a Chinese character which implies submissiveness or yielding. However this is not to be confused with weakness, but is more in keeping with the Taoist concept of yielding as applied to the martial arts. Jutsu is a Japanese term. It is generic and encompasses the multitude of combat systems indigenous to the Japanese . . e.ge., bajutsu refers to horsemanship; chikujo-jutsu refers to fortifications techniques; senjo-jutsu refers to warrior development.

As was the purpose of most Japanese martial arts, that of combative purposes, this new style of fighting was immediately incorporated into their military training program, and initially included kicking, striking, throwing, choking, and joint locking. Jujutsu reached its peak of development during the war periods and the late 17th century to the mid 19th century. This was often spoken of as the golden age of jujutsu. However, after the war periods, jujutsu, like everything else that outlives necessity, was downgraded and fell into decline. The many excellent warriors were no longer in demand and once released from the military, began teaching and giving

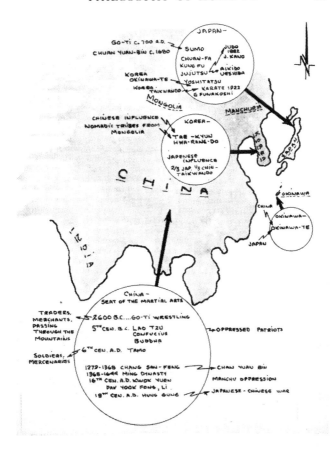

demonstrations in order to wrestle out a living. At this time, c. late 19th century, Jujutsu nearly vanished completely, and evolved into a form of sport and public amusement.

In 1882, Jigoro Kano, an expert in Jujutsu, recognizing the danger of perpetuating the deadly art to the public, modified it by eliminating many of the breaks and throws. He also deleted the kill and combative aspects, along with many of the weapons forms, (and) took the remains and developed his system of Judo. And so, jujutsu, without the hard combative elements as breaking and killing, by the early 20th century became the Japanese national sport of Judo and Jigoro Kano was acclaimed its founder.

Even though Jujutsu did fall into obscurity, it is well worth noting the importance it played as the precursor of two offshoot systems of Japanese self defense, ... not only Judo, but also another system which was to become equally famous. . . . Aikido.

Aikido is a Japanese art system that was instituted by M. Ueshiba. Its physical aspect included grasping and throwing indigenous to the Chinese "che-na" style. But more than that, Aikido was a blending of the physical with the mental and spiritual, and now we have in Japan the development of a complete martial arts system. . . . or more . . . the development of an art.

M. Ueshiba had studied many of the existing martial arts systems, and recognized that as a complete art, what existed at that time was lacking. He recognized that the element of spiritual development was obviously deleted from the system, and so he decided to develop his own style. He used as a basis for this new style, aiki-jutsu, which had been known for centuries in Japan. This style used as its basis, the development of the spiritual as well as the physical aspects. Up to this time, the style had not gained many followers. Ueshiba expanded the principles of aiki-jutsu and with modifications established a system dependent on the utilization of the opponent's force. It was a concept of natural rhythm, consisting of a free flowing personal expeience which offered no conflict to the laws of nature.

It is not difficult to see the relationship of his philosophy to the doctrines of Taoism and Buddhism and therefore to Kung Fu. It is a recorded historical fact that during the development of his style, he traveled to China to learn more of the Chinese systems as well as the Chinese philosophy. It would appear that Usehiba did, in fact, incorporate many of the philosophical doctrines of the Chinese as well as many of the physical principles and utilized these as the core of his revolutionary art.

Finally, in 1942, Ueshiba, using aiki-jutsu as a foundation, and the Chinese concept of philosophy and che-na as complimentary pedestals, presented to the world, his mature, modified martial arts system of Aikido.

The next system of consideration, which developed from the impetus of Chinese self defense is Karate.

Karate, is of course, not indigenous to Japan, but rather is a product of Okinawa, and was introduced to Japan in 1922, by Gichen Funakoshi.

Okinawa is the main island of the Ryukyu Island chain in the East China Sea. From very ancient times, it was always in close contact with both Japan and China. Initially, most of the information on fighting techniques infiltrated from China during the late sixteenth and early seventeenth century. Up to this time the Ryukyus had little or no martial arts ability. During this period, China had decided to replace many of her civilian envoys with military men, many of whom were knowledgeable and proficient fighters. Once in Okinawa, these men began teaching the townspeople many of the techniques of Chuan-fa or Kung-Fu. The people, thirsting for this type of information, absorbed it as quickly as they could and became very adept at the Chinese style. Eventually they added the Okinawan characteristics and produced a system they called Okinawa-te.

Later in the 17th century, Okinawa was invaded and defeated by Japan and was destined to exist under Japanese oppression for almost three hundred years. Immediately the Japanese outlawed weapons and empty hand fighting. The Okinawans hated their oppressors and being an ingenious race continued to develop the empty hand system of Okinawa-te underground. Not only did empty hand fighting develop to a high degree, but also the people devised a multitude of weapons out of seemingly harmless farm implements such as the "bo" or staff, the "kama" or sickle, and the "nun-chaku" or rice beater. And now the Okinawans had a complete self-defense system against their hated oppressors.

Finally, Okinawa was completely assimilated by Japan between 1890-1940, and so started an exchange of knowledge between the two countries. Okinawa-te found its way to Japan and Judo and Jujutsu were introduced to Okinawa.

In 1869, Gichin Funakoshi was born in Shuri, Okinawa. He began practicing the martial arts at age eleven, and in time became a Karate expert. In 1922, he was invited to give a demonstration in Japan at a physical education exposition. He so impressed the emperior Horohito, that by 1932, Karate became a part of the educational system of Japan. Finally Okinawa-te, combined with many of the Japanese elements, such as Jujutsu, and the end result was the Japanese system of Karate that we know today.

The word Karate itself is a study in history. Karate is the Japanese pronunciation of two Chinese characteristics . . . Kara and te. . . . which are literally translated to mean empty hand.

Kara was one of the old provinces in China, which was responsible for unifying all of the old country. During the period of the Kara Kingdom, much of the martial arts information leaked out to many satellite countries, such as Japan, Korea and Okinawa. Hence these techniques were referred to as the hand of the Kara Kingdom or the Kara hand. Only recently was Kara hand or Kara-te, changed to empty hand in Japanese terminology.

The last country we will discuss that exemplifies the exportation of Chinese self-defense and the changes it underwent is Korea.

Korea, being near Manchuria, in North East China was first exposed to the art by Chinese Buddhist monks from the northern mountains, and later by traveling merchants. They absorbed the art form, modified it and adapted it to their own topography and philosophy as did most of the other countries receiving the seeds of self defense. The Koreans, being a naturally strong legged people, as owing to their mountains, hilly, rocky terrain, favored the foot and leg techniques. They combined these new forms with their own system, thus producing a very unique Korean interpretation of martial art.

Aside from the Chinese influence, the Korean style which was indigenous to the land can be traced back more than 2000 years. At that time, the Korean warriors, a group of knights and nobles, had developed a martial arts style evolved out of an ancient kicking exercise which the Koreans called tae kyun. One group of these nobles in particular, were the Hwa-Rang-Do, a self appointed group of honorable knights who fought courageously to protect the people from oppression and injustice. However as the system outlived its need, much of the original art was lost to history, and very little of the original style exists today. Even though the system as a whole declined, much of the foot techniques continued to be practiced both as a sport and as a self defense system.

Further decline of the art occurred when Japan occupied Korea in 1910 and for 36 years much of the Japanese was absorbed by the Koreans. As time elapsed, many of the old masters passed on, thus losing more of the original art form, and now the younger Koreans were learning directly or indirectly from the Japanese instructors. Now the Korean style became 2/3 Japanese and 1/3 Chinese, and was called Tae-Kwon-Do which was a blending of the Korean Hwa-Rang-Do and the Japanese Karate. The style took on obvious Japanese characteristics except that the Koreans favored the use of feet. Literally, the word Tae-Kwon-Do is derived from the Korean "Tae" meaning to kill or smash with the foot, "Kwon" meaning to destroy with the hand or fist and "Do" referring to an art or method.

The end of World War II brought an end to Japan's 36 year occupation of Korea. Beyond that, World War II was responsible for disseminating the seeds of the martial arts throughout the world. Servicemen from afar, particularly American servicemen, were, for the first time in history exposed to the mysteries of oriental self-defense, Chinese philosophy, and the whole, broad exciting culture of the orient. Once the seed was planted, it grew and blossomed and swept through America with so much enthusiasm that today there are millions of devotees who practice self-defense as an avocation.

Until very recently Chinese self defense has not grown with the same rapidity as other martial arts systems. The reasons for this will be discussed in the next chapter. Suffice it to say, that finally, the Chinese people have decided to share their vast repository of knowledge and culture with the world, and now the tide of Chinese self defense is slowly gaining momentum. Within the next decade, Chinese self defense specifically, Kung Fu, will overshadow most of the other existing styles, and will truly be recognized as the mother source of all self defense systems.

The slow growth of Kung Fu, the reasons for its slow growth, and the many ramifications of this theme will be discussed in the next chapter.

Transmigration of Kung Fu

618-907. .Tang Dynasty. .the "Go-ti" dance found its way to Japan and becomes the foundation for Japanese Sumo wrestling, the national sport of Japan.

1368-1648. .Ming Dynasty. .when the Manchu invaded China, the art went underground. Chan Yuan-bin, a Ming patriot, took refuge in the Bushin Temple in Tokyo to teach Zen, meditation and Kung Fu. One of his pupils, Miura Yoshitatsu, became extremely adept and used this knowledge to develop his own system of Jujutsu.

c. 1850. . As the war period declined in Japan, so too did the need for such an offensive system, and so Jutjutsu fell into decline. By the late 19th century, it survived only in the form of a sport and public amusement.

1869. . . . .Gichen Funakoshi. .born in Okinawa. He began practicing the martial arts at age eleven and became the first Okinawa-te expert. In 1922, he demonstrated his art to the Japanese emperor and by 1932 Okinawa-te was modified with many of the Japanese elements and became the Japanese system of Karate.

1882. . . . .Jigoro Kano. .deleted many of the kill aspects of Jujutsu and formed his system of Judo.

1894-1895...Chinese-Japanese War..China in the peace settlement forfeits Korea and Okinawa to Japan, and so much of the Chinese fighting techniques was absorbed by the Japanese.

1910.....Japan occupies Korea and inculcated into the Korean system of Hua-Rang-do, much of the Japanese character, thus making it two thirds Japanese and one third Chinese. The result was the system of Kai-Kwan-do.

1930.....M. Usehiba.. developed his own system Aiki-jutsu. However, recognized it as an incomplete art lacking the spiritual aspect. He therefore traveled to China seeking that unknown, and in 1942, employing Aiki-jutsu as the foundation and the Chinese concepts of philosophy as its compliment, presented to Japan and to the world his mature system of Aikido.

The Slow Growth of Kung-Fu
Outside China

Why is it that Kung-Fu, which is such a dynamic and complete martial arts system, and in effect the mothersource of all other martial arts systems, did not gain any momentum outside of China for many years? In fact, not until very recently has the term Kung-Fu become part of the American vocabulary, and this mostly due to the exploitation of the commercial media, specifically movies and television.

The reasons are as complex as they are many, but I have narrowed them down to the following: first of all there has always been an innate ideology of secrecy or family unity or even nationalism which has dominated the Chinese mind; secondly for many centuries there has been a distrust and even a hatred amongst the Chinese for all foreigners; and finally the concepts of the teaching or rather the teachers themselves. To express these thoughts in one word, the reasons for the slow growth of Chinese culture, philosophy and knowledge as a whole is a reflection of the Chinese attitude.

I often wonder if the Great Wall of China was built to resist the onslaught of the barbarian tribes, or rather to keep in the wisdom of Chinese culture which to them represents years of precious heritage belonging to no one but themselves.

The ideology of unity and/or secrecy has always played a very important part of Chinese civilization. In the family unit, due respect was always afforded the elder. All family activity orientated around the elders and their opinion on all matters was law. Even in the villages and communities, the elders were considered sages and were held in high esteem. They often formed a council and decided all matters of social, political and domestic significance.

Through years of wars and anarchy, this concept of unity amongst families and villages was reinforced and out of this grew the need for closeness and even secrecy within these small clusters.

During the Boxer Rebellion, the Chinese developed a hatred for all foreigners and this feeling has persisted to this day. In mainland China, it is almost impossible to pierce the "Bamboo Curtain" without such a tremendous amount of political arbi-

The Great Wall of China not only resisted foreign invasion but also contained the Chinese culture.

tration, that it is obvious the Chinese are saying to the world, "stay away foreigners, we don't want you here, leave us alone."

Is-so-far-as this concept touched on every phase of family life, it is not difficult to see how it affected the martial arts. In its embryonic stages, Kung-Fu, after it had escaped the confines of the monastaries was kept between families as part of their heritage. It was generally learned by one member of the family and then taught to the other members. In this way the secrets of the art were kept within the family and passed on from generation to generation. Unfortunately, often the last member of a family might have been a disinterested member who did not wish to perpetuate the art and so many of the secrets died with him.

In many cases, a small community would consist of a population that was interrelated and so Kung-Fu would be taught to the entire village. Often a village with no knowledge of the art, would hire a professional fighter to come and teach them Kung-Fu and in this way the village would be able to protect itself from bandits, barbarians and dynastic oppressions. Eventually as many villages developed champions, tournaments were held in which one village would challenge another. Because of a strong feeling of pride within each village, many of the secret styles they had learned or developed were closely guarded secrets, and so the ideology of secrecy or unity was perpetuated within the villages and families themselves.

Following this line of reasoning, it is not too difficult to see why the Chinese are not inclined to share their heritage with each other. How much less are they eager to share their secrets with foreigners, whom they have grown to hate; initially the occupational forces of the Manchu, then the occupational

forces of Japan and finally after the turn of the twen-
tieth century, all the foreigners who were attempting
to exploit a weakened and disunified China. Why
China has elected to remain an isolated countries, and
is not too eager to solicit relationships with any other
countries, even those with whom she shares social
or political bonds, is no great mystery.

It is well worth noting that the art of Kung-Fu
which has recently spread throughout the world has
not leaked out of mainland China, but rather from
the Chinese who were either driven out or those who
fled the Communist takeover of mainland China, i.e.,
those who fled to satellite areas such as Hong Kong or
to the Republic of China, Taiwan. These are the men
to whom we are indebted for having shared with us
their knowledge of Kung-Fu. Much of the art also has
been brought to us by servicemen of the World War
II era. Also during the post war days, many of the
Chinese themselves immigrated to foreign lands and
those that did brought with them the secrets of the
art.

The Chinese teachers themselves, have in many
cases represented an obstacle to the growth of Kung
Fu in our country. The teachers fall into three
categories and are worth considering in order to develop our theme.

First there are many excellent Chinese teachers
who have elected to settle in Chinese communities in
the United States. Many of these men restrict their
teaching to only Chinese students. In many cases
Americans wishing to take lessons are either turned
away or are taught an entirely different level of self
defense.

Secondly, there are many teachers who, out of
economics, have elected to teach Americans and to
this end have established schools. However oftentime,

the knowledge that is taught is limited and orientated around health and hygiene rather than self defense.

Finally, the last category of teachers . . . . the true master, who sincerely wishes to perpetuate the art and establish a base of Chinese Kung-Fu here in the United States. This man realizes that with no knowledge of the art, one can never really appreciate Kung-Fu, and so will never be able to maintain a true perspective of Chinese self defense in relation to Japanese, Korean etc, martial arts and inevitably, like the perpetuation of Kung-Fu from one generation to another, the art will be partially or totally lost. This man is interested in teaching the art, he is definitely interested in developing fighters with both the knowledge and ability to compete with all or any of the other martial arts systems and ultimately to show the world not only the effectiveness of Kung-Fu but also the beauty that it reflects.

Another factor that has hindered the growth of Kung-Fu is the Chinese concept of humility and softness. Following the philosophy of Tao, the true Chinese master does not try to impress the world with his feats of strength and bulkiness of muscle. The American image of manhood generally envisions the Charles Atlas type of man, with massive chest development and rippling biceps; a man who fears nothing and lets everyone know it; a man who speaks boldly and proclaims his place in life.

As mentioned earlier, the Way of Lao Tzu is the way of softness in which the weak overcomes the strong and the soft overcomes the hard. Because of its impression of yielding and submissiveness, Taoism initially lost many followers who believed Confucianism to be more manly. This concept still prevails. Most of the true Chinese masters carry an air of humility and quietude, rather than an air of bravado

. . . . . they appear not aggressive but submissive . . . . not hard, but soft, . . . not outer musculature, but inner strength. This in contrast to the yelling, screaming Karate student, flying through the air, muscles rippling, crashing through boards, is not overly impressive to the untrained American eye. But as of late and again because of the commercial media, the American public is becoming more aware of the depth of softness, submissiveness and yielding. Also the American public is becoming more aware of the deficiencies and limitations of the totally hard system of training.

As mentioned in an earlier chapter, the merits of a strict hard training system is relatively short lived. In the circle of martial arts with which I am acquainted, I know many young men who can no longer practice the hard style because of injured knees, knuckles and backs. I have heard it said that some of the older practicioners of the hard style used to break their knuckles purposely and let the bone fuse into one massive striking area. Many of these devotees eventually suffer arthritis of many of these joints and are restricted in their ability to practice.

In other competitive areas such as football and baseball, we are all familiar with the relatively short productive life span of our athletes. As we all know, the effectiveness of the hard style is dependent on speed and strength. Unfortunately, everyone ages and these characteristics decline. Hence once the speed decreases and the musculature deteriorates, so too does the ability to effectively practice deteriorate.

This is the beauty of Kung Fu. Though it does encompass many of the hard elements, there is a balance with the soft . . . because the purpose of the art is health and longevity and as such is meant to be practiced throughout one's life.

Because of the unwillingness of the Chinese, until recently, to show their proficiency in tournament fighting as well was being limited because of the point system (i.e., many of the lethal strikes are disallowed and many others are not scored as points), Kung-Fu has received little tournament exposure. Because of this "poor showing" in tournaments, which are a measure of the martial arts in the United States, Chinese Schools have become recognized as a haven of kata or form, and as such "apparently ineffective" as a system of self defense.

The last reason for the slow growth of Kung Fu outside of China, is once again the result of the Chinese attitude . . . specifically, the methods of teaching. In general, the true Chinese teachers are a product of the ancient methods of teaching. In the old days when a person wished to learn Kung-Fu, he would present himself to the house of the master and await an audience. Oftentime, he would return day after day remaining at the front door for many hours. Finally, he would be allowed within the home and relegated a series of menial tasks which he was expected to discharge with humility and proficiency. This process may have evolved over a period of many weeks or months. And then, one day, he was asked to appear before the master and his training would begin. The training itself was a long arduous process. He was expected to give totally of himself and then more. He was expected to hold exhaustingly painful positions for long periods of time, asking no questions. He was expected to practice movements until in the master's eyes they were perfect and only then was he given more information. For example, one complete form would probably involve a year of study by the student. In general, the training period often extended over twenty years.

But again, this was the Chinese mind . . . . one of patience and humility. Equating this to the typical American student, one can easily see why Kung-Fu has not flourished. For one thing, in ancient China, a master was not generally paid in dollars and cents. The student would honor the master with favors, or services and particularly with respect. In the United States, a student pays for the services, and so expects a return which is measurable by his own standards. Therefore he questions every aspect of teaching, rather than wait till he himself can see the answers; also and of most importance, the typical American is an impetuous creature and does not expect to spend twenty years to perfect Kung-Fu. Unless he is taught something new at each session he becomes quickly discouraged and does not fail to reproach his teacher. To learn real Kung Fu, a student must be willing to spend much time in practice. He must work very hard developing exercises which will strengthen him and thus enable him to perform the necessary movements correctly and with ease. He must be willing to devote many hours studying the philosophy which encompasses the art of Kung-Fu and so better understand the art as a whole rather than ineffectively develop only one aspect of the art and therefore only one aspect of himself. Kung-Fu cannot be learned in a month or a year . . . but is the result of a lifetime of study and of exercise . . . . everrefining . . . . ever perfecting . . . ever developing in the pure sense of the word . . . the complete art of Kung Fu.

In conclusion, the reasons for the slow growth of Kung-Fu outside of China is a direct result of the Chinese mind, specifically his attitude. His attitude towards his ancient heritage, his attitude towards foreigners, and finally his attitudes on teaching. Very slowly over many years all of these concepts have undergone some degree of attrition, and finally the doors of Kung-Fu are slowly but still cautiously being opened to the world. To what degree the Chinese will trust the foreigners with their heritage and wisdom is unknown. Only time can tell whether or not the Chinese will completely open the doors to the vast repository of experience and wisdom that he has acquired to the martial arts system . . . . and more to ancient Chinese culture as a whole.

The Commercial Ramifications of Kung Fu

Yes . . . the martial arts are here to stay. Like the
onrush of a tidal wave, the martial arts have swept the
country and from all appearances will become as
much an institution in the American way of life as
baseball and football. Initially looked upon as a violent sport, attracting only low class and low income
devotees, the martial arts have been greatly tempered
and modified so that it has appeal to all and any class
of people. More and more each day Kung Fu schools
are becoming a haven for professional people and
high level educated people as well. This is due to the
flexibility of the martial arts, which offer not only self
defense, but also health, peace of mind, philosophy
and a whole wide range of tangent interests as well.
Also the arts have been given tremendous impetus by
the commercial world in the form of television,
newspapers and movies.

The fastest growing of the martial arts in the past
decade has been Karate. Even though Karate is an
offshoot of Kung Fu, it has gained a tremendous following for many reasons. First of all is the appeal of
the fiery, flashy, board breaking, brick busting aspect
of the art which cannot be less than impressive. Also
there is a lack of good Chinese instructors and instruction for reasons mentioned in the previous chapter. And finally a nationwide movement by the commercial world who always capitalizes on what appears
to be the most sensational aspect of the martial arts.

Initially, big industry was unaware of the sleeping
giant that was the martial arts. With the introduction
of the Television Kung Fu Series, the nation was
proded into an awareness, and the dam was broken.

The movie industry flooded theatres with martial arts films theoretically exhibiting the merits of Chinese Kung Fu, but actually extolling the style of Karate; Five Fingers of Death, Fists of Fury, Enter the Dragon, The Screaming Tiger, Duel of the Iron Fists, etc. Initially Hong Kong produced most of these films. Finally Hollywood saw the rising success of these films and strated production in the United States. Theoretically, the movie industry has plans for another 5.7 years of production before it feels a saturation point has been reached. Magazines have added to the impetus of growing interest in the martial arts . . . . Black Belt, Karate Illustrated, Fighting Stars, Kung Fu etc. The interest has been augmented by more exposure by Television sports shows, which are now showing tournament and form exhibitions. Also more and more talk shows have added to the exposure by featuring as guests, martial art teachers and performers, thus adding to the public more knowledge of the martial arts. Even though the commercialism of Kung Fu is many times distorted, and oftentimes untrue, it has at least opened the public eye and planted the seed of curiosity . . . . and for this we should be thankful.

Only recently, has the influence of Chinese self defense been noticeable. Until a few short years ago, Kung Fu was equated with Karate, was equated with TaiKwando, was equated with Judo etc. Because of this reasoning, many unqualified people were attempting to teach Kung Fu. For example many Karate schools, who for years have taught Karate, and whose names have become almost synonomous with Karate are attempting to take advantage of the surge of Chinese self defense and have merely added Kung Fu to their advertising, even though they lack trained instructors. Also, as in the embryonic stages of Karate, Kung Fu schools are opening on every corner of every city extolling their abilities and certificates. And as always, the untrained innocent public must make its decision as to which instructors are qualified and which are not.

Even amongst the qualified Chinese instructors there are differences in the type of instruction offered. Remembering that Kung Fu at its inception was a form of health and hygiene, this attitude is upheld by many teachers, and so these schools adhere to the health and exercise aspects of Kung Fu. In China today, there are literally thousands of people who, each day at a prescribed time, go to the local square and proceed through a series of exercises and forms designed to promote health and hygiene. Continuing, some masters teach only kata or form, feeling that expertise in form leads to expertise in self defense. Initially forms were construed to disguise a series of self defense manuevers and in this way could be passed through generations without revealing the secret implications of the movements. However many of these beautiful and purposeful forms have deteriorated throughout the years and in many cases remain as a ballet, calesthenic like dance. On the other hand many of these forms remain true to their purpose and serve as an excellent teaching aid to self defense, poise, balance and timing.

Further, there are excellent Chinese teachers who devote their classes purely to the philosophy of Kung Fu which is an entire study in itself. The sketchy outline we have presented just touches the tip of the abysmall reservoir of ancient Chinese philosophy which in itself is a life long study.

Finally, there is the true master who teaches Kung Fu as the whole complete art that it is, and so trains the student as a whole being, mentally, physically and spiritually and in this way is perpetuating the true art. It is not the intent of the true master to teach only self defense . . . or to teach only philosophy . . . or to teach only health and hygiene . . . . but rather to develop the student in all three areas . . . slowly, deliberately and effectively. The true master does not wish to produce an effective fighting machine capable of winning tournaments and filling the school with trophies, but rather to produce a complete human being capable of seeing far beyond the immediate results of physical strength and reaches for the long range effectiveness of peace, tranquility, health and longevity. For this reason it should be realized that there is no such thing as instant Kung Fu. But rather, to develop the art effectively requires much time, patience and especially hard work.

As always there is a product for every demand, whether buying an automobile, clothing or instruction in Kung Fu . . . . and in making a purchase, the same principle holds true . . "Caveat Emptor." In other words, it is up to the student to decide what he wants out of the martial arts and then find qualified instruction. That is, does he merely want to learn how to break bricks and boards; is he interested in free sparring; is he interested in winning tournaments; is he interested in self-defense; or is he interested in learning the complete art of Kung Fu along with the philosophical principles and culture of the ancients?

Secondly, he must seek out qualified instruction that will lead him to his objectives. Most reputable schools will allow a prospective student to attend one or two classes at no charge to the student. There should be no big secret about what is being taught in class. The potential student should attend at least one or more classes to determine whether or not this school will satisfy his needs.

Finally he must realize that there is no way any student can become proficient overnight. He must be willing to spend many hours over a long period of time not only taking instruction but also practicing on his own, before he is able to perform what he is learning effectively. The American mind tends to equate knowledge in terms of quantity rather than quality. This axion, however, does not apply to the martial arts . . . because in truth, it matters little how much one knows, but rather how well one can execute what he knows.

The commercial world in general is capable of presenting, much too often, a production in an ambiguous light. Much too often the consumer presents a product to the public which does not live up to its expectations. In seeking Kung Fu instruction, it is up to the individual to intelligently and rationally investigate all the ramifications, before committing himself. In this way, he will be happy with his choice and the master will be happy with a satisfied student who knows exactly where he is going.

Epilogue

Generally the dedication of a book is found in the preface. However, I have reserved my dedication until the end because I feel that this epilogue is so very meaningful to my wife Konnie, who has been inspirational throughout this writing and to my three lovely children, Earline, Laurie, and Nicki, who are always in my heart. And now the epilogue:

Before turning the last page of this book, I would like to discuss one last and probably the most important aspect of Kung Fu.

Up to now, we have traced the evolution of Kung Fu from its philosophical and religious foundations. We have seen the influence of the many factors that helped mold Kung Fu, such as the thousands of pre-existing fighting forms and styles, the socio-political pressures which drove the art underground and gave it a tone of esotericism, and the impact of religious forces as Buddhism, Confucianism, and Taoism. Like the river of which Holmes Welch speaks, we have seen many streams flow into it at its inception . . . and at its delta we see the river split into numerous tributaties such as Karate, Judo, Tai-Kwando, Aikido, etc., Kung Fu as a fighting art is all of these . . . . . that is what is so beautiful about the system. It is punching . . . it is kicking . . . . it is grasping and throwing. Kung Fu is the system most closely resembling the original art form practiced by the ancient Chinese masters. Truly, it is the mother source of all martial art.

But more than this, what does Kung Fu mean to the development of man? What does it add to the incomplete, ever-searching soul of man?

Yes . . . . man will forever be man . . . . driven by a

compulsive instinct to excel, pressing ever forward towards the unreachable quest, pursuing that intangible which he cannot see, that which he cannot define, that which he cannot understand, and that which in his lifetime he will probably never know. Yet he pushes on and on, attempting to grasp the elusive quintessence .... to gain just a glance of it. As Buddha states, man spends his life in pursuit of the intimate happiness and once having achieved it watches its luster disappear and then repeats the endless cycle of desire and attainment. Woe to ye mankind, forever wretched, forever frustrated, forever striving, forever straining ... forever reaching to the heavens and when finally, the end is within reach .... it is gone.

Then what is it man is seeking ... what is it that drives man ever forward? What is it that pervades his reason and causes him to forsake everything, relentlessly pressing forward?

Unfortunately, man is ego, and looks outward, beyond himself for answers, looking only to satisfy his ego. Fame, fortune, success .... all are products of the ego, and so offer only a limited degree of happiness. Eternal happiness on the other hand lies within the heart of man. It invokes an understanding of the ego, and therefore an understanding of self. All the great philosophers throughout civilization have given us this message.

The oracle at Delphi admonished the world with this message, "Know Thyself."

Christ told us, "For how does it help a man to gain the whole world and yet lose his immortal soul."

Lao Tzu in the Tao Te Ching said,
"But why you know
what eternally is so,
you have stature.

And stature means righteousness
and righteousness is kingly,
and kingly divine.
And divinity is the Way
Which is final.

Confucius said, "If a man can for one day master himself . . . . . . all under heaven will return to humanity."

And finally the doctrine of Zen (ch'an), tells us that the kingdom of heaven lies in the heart of man . . . though it turns inward, it radiates outward. It does not speak of a supreme being which demands obedience with promises of life everlasting or the punishment of the pains of hell. Nor does it speak of a God who has spoken to only a chosen few . . . leaving in his wake dogmas and tablets having supernatural powers. There is only one God and that is the God within each man . . . it is the God of wisdom, knowledge and truth, thereby making each man responsible for life and living.

This is the message of the sages . . . that is the "Great Doctrine," this is the truth of life . . . . and to know the truth is to know oneself . . . . . and to know oneself is to know God . . . for God is within us. Truth is good . . . . . truth is purpose . . . truth is life. Each man must find his own . . . and then live it . . . no matter what the cost.

"To thine own self be true
And it must follow as the
    night and the day.
Thou canst not then be
    false to any man."

But how does one find the truth . . . how does one grasp the "Great Doctrine"? The search is a long and arduous one . . . . taking many years, much work and in many cases continual failure and frustration. To completely understand the implications, it is necessary to return to the Shaolin Temple of the ancients in which the primary objective was truth, and Kung Fu was only a means to that end. Zen Buddhists utilized many different arts as a means, such as flower arranging, the tea ceremony, archery and painting. Each of these arts represents a discipline which has as its objective not the perfection of the art, but rather a means to a higher end . . . that of emptying oneself. The art itself becomes purposeless or aimless or the true objective is lost.

As with man's life cycle . . . . he becomes so involved with the pressures of everyday living, that he continually pushes and presses with so much fervor that the real objective of life is lost. And once he has achieved his imaginary goals, the joy is short lived and the cycle begins again. The line of reasoning is this . . . the arts are not meant to be an end in themselves and therefore must never be forced. As long as man continues to press he will never discover the real truth. Hence because his mind is filled with an unreal objective, he must be aware of this and utilize the arts as they were meant to be used. . . . as a spiritual exercise or, discipline, which presupposes a spiritual attitude as it were, through which he may accomplish victory not outwardly but inward within himself.

Hence, the art itself must be purposeless, effortless and aimless to that . . . it just happens. The more one presses, the less one succeeds. It becomes analagous to threading a needle in which purpose tremor becomes a factor . . . or the centipede who was unable to move once he thought about which foot to move first. The arts become a vehicle for developing within oneself total emptiness through which develops a increased acuteness of the senses or rather the development of an extra sense. This extra sense, this emptiness is the first step towards discovery of the inner self . . . . the inner truth . . . the "Great Doctrine".

This then is the real purpose of Kung Fu. It is not the breaking of bricks or the crushing of bones, but rather the purpose of Kung Fu is as a spiritual exercise or discipline through which one may establish a pattern for life. It becomes a vehicle for uniting man with nature . . . with the universe . . . this union should be natural and unopposed so that one may lose himself effortlessly and thereby become purposeless. In this way man discovers within himself an inner peace, an inner calmness, an inner serenity so that we may better live with ourselves and with others. It brings us a step closer to truth and hence the real meaning of life . . . . . who can ask for more?

The order of things in nature is cyclical . . . the day draws to a close with dusk, then descends into night, only to be reborn again with the dawn, ascending again to the brilliance of day to repeat the never ending cycle.

Life is but the sum of all the laws of nature . . . a series of comings and goings. Indeed life is the study of nature . . and nature the study of life. Each represents a harmonious balance of smooth flowing predictable transmutations in which all things find their place and all contradictions and diversities are resolved into one unity. In this orderly universe, the life cycle of man, the majestic order of the seasons, the skies, the mountains . . . all are the way of the Tao. These laws are imbodied in every man, every rock, every star. In the end, the Tao and life become one.

All that is, follows this smooth endless cycle of predictable events. The seasons undergo the same imperceptable changes . . . spring into summer; summer into autumn; and finally autumn into winter. With the changing seasons, flowers too, follow the natural law of cyclical transmutation. They come into being, fulfill their destiny, and then, reaching full bloom, return to the source from whence they came.

And finally man himself, who is but an infinitesimal part of this magnificent universe, is subject to the same laws . . . he is born of nothingness, then like the cyclical seasons, undergoes a series of changes, living out his life . . . and then passes asleep . . . . forever.

To deny this is to deny destiny . . . for this is the natural way . . . this is the way of life . . . this is the way of the Tao . . . . ..